Beat the Course, Not Yourself!

One Golfer's Path to a Winning Mental Game

GARY CHRISTIAN
&
DR. CURT ICKES

Copyright © 2024 by Dr. Curt Ickes & Gary Christian

First Paperback Edition: 2024.

All rights reserved. No part of this book may be used or reproduced in any form or by any electronic or mechanical means, including information storage and retrieval systems—except in the case of brief quotations embodied in critical articles or reviews, without written permission from its authors and publisher. Printed in the United States.

Beat The Course LLC
Ashland, OH 44805

ISBN: 9798300907020
Published by KDP

Edited by: Cynthia Hilston
Cover Illustration by: Russell Gunning

Beat the Course, Not Yourself!
A Golfer's Path to a Winning Mental Game

Golf isn't just about physical skill; it's about mastering your mind, too. In *Beat the Course, Not Yourself!*, former PGA Tour player Gary Christian and bestselling sport psychologist Dr. Curt Ickes team up to equip you with the mental game strategies needed to elevate your play.

Jack Sullivan, a determined fifteen-year-old golfer, dreams of earning a college scholarship and playing professionally. But when the pressure's on, Jack's game falls apart. Then he meets Charlie, a seasoned pro whose battle-tested wisdom teaches Jack that true victory starts from within—by mastering focus, silencing doubt, and building a strategic pre-shot routine.

Blending real-world golf strategies with mental mastery, this compelling story delivers practical lessons that every golfer—especially young players—can apply right away. **From defeating negative self-talk to building a rock-solid pre-shot routine, *Beat the Course, Not Yourself!* is packed with actionable advice to transform your game.** Join Jack on his journey and discover how you, too, can stay calm, confident, and in control—even in the most intense moments.

Whether preparing for your next tournament or sharpening your daily practice, this book equips you with the tools to play your best.

Perfect for golfers at any level, you'll find out how to:

- Stay focused when the round doesn't go as planned
- Build a consistent pre-shot routine for more reliable results
- Boost your confidence and trust your swing when it counts
- Bounce back quickly after a bad shot or tough round
- Stay calm and handle pressure during competition
- Set clear goals and track your progress
- Build mental resilience to face any challenge

Beat the Course, Not Yourself! isn't just another golf book—it's your guide to mastering confidence, focus, and mental resilience, no matter what challenges the course may throw your way.

ABOUT THE AUTHORS

With over thirty years of experience, **Gary Christian** brings a wealth of knowledge—from his All-SEC days at Auburn University to thirty mini-tour victories and two Korn Ferry Tour titles. At age forty, Gary became one of the oldest rookies in PGA Tour history, a true testament to his commitment to mastering the mental game. He is now a PGA of America member and golf analyst for Golf Channel, ESPN, and PGA Tour Live. As a coach, Gary specializes in teaching players physical and mental game skills, as well as course management strategies.

Bestselling author and professor emeritus **Dr. Curt Ickes** has over thirty-five years of expertise in clinical and sport psychology. He has worked with athletes from youth leagues to the pros, helping them sharpen their mental game for peak performance. Dr. Ickes is known for his engaging storytelling and practical mental game strategies. His books—including *Win the Next Pitch!*, *Pitch by Pitch!*, and *You Got This!*—have collectively sold over 50,000 copies, helping thousands of athletes build mental toughness and succeed on and off the field.

Table of Contents

Forewords ix

Acknowledgements xiii

Chapter 1 – Am I Ready? 1

Chapter 2 – A Tale of Two Nines 11

Chapter 3 – The Old Pro's Secret 21

Chapter 4 – The Routine: A Golfer's Secret Weapon 29

Chapter 5 – What You Do Between Shots Matters 35

Chapter 6 – The Building Blocks of Success 41

Chapter 7 – Set Up and Let It Go! 49

Chapter 8 – Focused Practice Makes the Game Routine 53

Chapter 9 – Taking It to the Course 61

Chapter 10 – Relax Your Body, Free Your Mind 71

Chapter 11 – The Power of Positive Self-Talk 79

Chapter 12 – Confidence Is Built on Preparation 87

Chapter 13 – Showtime: Perform When It Matters 93

Chapter 14 – This Changes Everything 105

About the Authors 111

Forewords

As the head men's golf coach at Auburn University, I have had the fortunate opportunity to learn from Gary Christian over the past fifteen years. Gary's work with golfers of all skill levels has been extraordinary, allowing them to evolve mentally while simultaneously receiving physical results. Through our conversations about the mental game, he has helped me grow as a coach and better help my players strive for excellence.

My goals every season are to develop young people and produce winners on and off the golf course. I've been extremely blessed to learn from some terrific people that have vast knowledge in the game of golf. Gary has been instrumental in finding intangibles that I carry over to my players each and every year. His simple, well-thought-out game plan on the mentality of the sport has been a tremendously valuable tool to help us develop our players in a way that guides them towards success. It was exceptionally rewarding to see the time and effort placed on our players' mental game be fulfilled with Auburn's win in the 2024 National Championship. It was one of my most satisfying victories in my collegiate coaching career.

I have always strived to recruit and develop players at the highest level. The physical skills the top juniors possess are attractive, but what separates them from others is their ability to have a high state of mind and incredible mindset. *Beat the Course, Not Yourself!* is a wonderful introduction to learning and developing the necessary mental skills required in the game of golf. It's a simple, concise read and easy to follow along the pathway of the importance of a strong mental game. It will help you evaluate the way you think on the course and give you a good game plan on how to improve. You will think better and play with more confidence, which will ultimately lead to better scores. The importance of one's mental state on the golf course cannot be overstated, and this tremendous book helps one not forget it.

Enjoy the read and thank you Gary for all your guidance over the years!

Nick Clinard
Head Men's Golf Coach
Auburn University
2024 D1 National Coach of the Year

* * *

In golf, as in life, the mental game often determines success. Talent and technique may bring you to the fairway, but it's focus, resilience, and mental toughness that carry you through the rough. This book you hold in your hands is a masterclass in mastering the mind—equipping you with the tools to stay composed, confident, and driven, no matter what challenges you face on the course.

Golf is a game of variables: unpredictable weather, tricky lies, or a single bad shot that could derail an entire round. But what separates the great from the good is their ability to stay present, trust their preparation, and embrace each challenge as an opportunity for growth.

What makes this book particularly profound is how it aligns with the principles of the American Development Model (ADM). ADM emphasizes holistic growth, encouraging young athletes to develop both physical and mental skills while fostering a lifelong love for the sport. Golf, when introduced early and taught effectively, can become a catalyst for personal development, shaping not only better players but well-rounded individuals.

The mental strategies detailed in this book are crucial for all stages of a golfer's journey. For young players they mirror the ADM's core values of building confidence, fostering resilience, and embracing challenges as opportunities to grow. Through structured goal-setting and an emphasis on process over outcome, youth are taught to approach the game with curiosity and adaptability—skills that transcend golf and prepare them for life's complexities.

This book doesn't just speak to competitive golfers aiming for peak performance. It recognizes the broader, lifelong journey of golf as a medium for continuous learning and personal growth. Adults and seasoned players will find its insights equally valuable, as they remind us that mastery of the mental game is an ever-evolving process. Golf's beauty lies in its timeless appeal, offering new challenges and lessons at every stage of life.

The parallels between the mental principles covered here and ADM's focus on whole-child development are clear: both seek to cultivate individuals who are equipped to thrive in any environment. Whether it's staying calm under the pressures of competition or simply finding joy in a well-executed shot, the tools offered in this book will benefit anyone, from those just beginning their golfing journey to those who've been playing for decades.

As you embark on this journey, remember: golf is a reflection of life. There will be moments of brilliance, times of struggle, and everything in between. What matters most is your ability to face each moment with courage, grace, and unwavering belief in your potential.

May this book inspire you to play the game with joy, passion, perseverance, and an unshakable mindset. Here's to thriving under pressure and discovering your best self—both on the course and in life.

Suzy Whaley
Past President PGA of America

Acknowledgements

As this book makes its way into the world, we want to take a moment to acknowledge those who made its pages possible. A book is never the creation of just one person; it comes to life through a harmonious blend of minds, voices, and encouragement. We wish to express our sincere gratitude to everyone who helped bring this story to life.

To Tim Buren: Your introduction led to the partnership behind this book and set this entire project in motion. We appreciate and value your friendship.

To our wives, Dianne and Kimberly: Thank you for your steadfast support throughout the highs and challenges of this creative process. Your patience, encouragement, and insightful feedback have been a steadfast source of strength and inspiration. We are deeply grateful for your help in bringing this book to life.

To Coach Nick Clinard and Suzy Whaley: Thank you for your kind words about the book.

To Mackenzie Sloane, Jack Poole, Luka Hebert, and Noah Dennis: Thank you for your honesty and your ability to describe your feelings and actions in competitive situations.

Finally, a heartfelt thank you to our editor, Cynthia Hilston. We appreciate your discerning eye and exceptional editing. Your edits polished the manuscript, giving it clarity, depth, and lasting impact.

To everyone who played a role in making this book a reality—thank you for being part of this incredible journey.

With heartfelt appreciation,
Curt Ickes & Gary Christian

CHAPTER 1

Am I Ready?

"Whoa! Watch out!" Jack's entire body tensed as a firm grip pulled him back–right before a golf cart whooshed past, whipping cold air across his face.

"Dude, that was way too close! Pay attention, man!" Matt's hold loosened, his eyes wide.

"Thanks. I was totally zoned out, thinking about today." Jack gasped, turning to face his best friend, his heart racing. "I owe you big time."

Jack took a deep breath, the bustle of the parking lot yanking him back to reality. The early morning chill sank into his skin, the buzz of golf carts and the shuffle of the crowd filling his ears as people moved toward the Willow Springs clubhouse.

Dew sparkled on the grass, the sun casting long shadows across the fairways as Jack slowed his steps. Eager chatter about the tournament swirled around him, feeding the surge of energy building in his chest. The weight of his golf bag tugged at his shoulders, a constant reminder of how much today meant. This wasn't just another Saturday. Today could change everything.

At fifteen, Jack felt a lot more pressure than most kids his age. Golf wasn't just a game for him — it was his shot at a scholarship, maybe even a pro career someday. Every time he stepped onto the course, it felt like the whole world was watching.

His parents poured their hopes, time, and money into his lessons, practices, and gear. The Grand Strand Invitational wasn't just any tournament—it drew the best high school players in Eastern South Carolina. Being invited was an honor, but now Jack had to prove he belonged.

"Big day, Jack," Matt said, his voice buzzing with excitement as they reached the clubhouse. He held a steaming cup of hot chocolate, its sweet aroma mixing with the crisp morning air.

Jack smiled at his best friend's round, freckled face. Even though Matt wasn't as skilled at golf, his steady support always boosted Jack's spirits. The boys had met while working at the local golf course. Now, if they weren't working, they were playing golf together.

Jack nodded, but his voice wavered as he replied, "It is. That's for sure." He took a deep breath, knowing this was his big chance. Winning here could grab the attention of college coaches, which was crucial for the scholarship he needed.

As Jack adjusted his hat, he knew one thing mattered the most: to beat these top players, he had to play his best.

Around him, the sounds of the golf course filled the air—the soft thuds of golf bags being set down, the clinks of clubs, and the hum of golf carts. The smell of freshly cut grass wafted on the soft breeze.

He scanned the crowd of competitors. "There are a lot of great golfers here," he said, still fidgeting with his cap.

"Yep, and you're one of them, Jack. You can win this," Matt said, his grin widening, eyes full of certainty.

"I hope so. We'll see," Jack muttered, doubt creeping into his voice.

Jack's gaze finally locked onto a familiar figure. A tall, blond boy stood laughing loudly with a group of golfers, waving his hands as he told a story.

"Great, there's Nick Sanders—always so cool and confident. Or should I say cocky? He knows the college coaches are watching him."

"Don't stress about Nick. He's not that great. You've beaten him before," Matt reassured, nodding at Jack.

"Just once. I've only beaten him once," Jack replied, eyes glued to his rival. "I came close other times but couldn't pull it off. I always fell apart at the end."

Jack's mind wandered back to last year when Jack unexpectedly beat Nick in a big high school match. Since then, Nick had beaten Jack every time. His smirks and smug attitude sent a clear message to Jack: He was superior. Every time it happened, Jack's self-doubt grew, and Nick's flawless swing seemed even more daunting.

"Today, you can beat him again. Just don't let Nick get under your skin," Matt encouraged.

Jack rubbed his face slowly, scanning the group. "The problem is, I'm surrounded by Nicks."

Just as Matt was about to reply, Nick's gaze pierced through the crowd, locking onto Jack. Nick, his head held high and with an extra bounce in his step, made his way over to the boys.

Nick folded his arms across his chest, puffing out slightly as if daring Jack to respond. "Well, well, if it isn't Sullivan. Back to try again, I see."

Jack's face heated. "What do you want, Nick?"

Nick's grin widened. "Oh, that's easy. I want to beat you and everyone else today. I'm confident I'll walk away the winner."

Nick's eyes traced Jack up and down, assessing every part of him. "You're looking scrawnier than the last time we played. How's that weak drive of yours? Still slicing them?"

Matt stepped forward, his face reddening. "Back off, Nick. Jack's ready, and you know it."

Nick chuckled. "Time will tell." He turned to leave, then paused and glanced back. "Oh, Jack, you might want to start doing your own talking." With that, he walked away, still grinning.

"What a loser. Don't let him get to you," Matt said. "His head is bigger than this whole course."

"Yeah," Jack replied, still watching Nick in the distance. "He's good, and he knows it. Do I really have what it takes to beat him?"

Matt took a slow sip of his hot chocolate, watching the steam curl into the cool air. "Yeah, buddy, yeah, you do..." His voice trailed off.

They watched quietly as other players gathered around Nick, seeking his attention. The awkward silence stretched out like the morning mist.

Jack had already warmed up on the range and was feeling confident, having hit most shots well. Still, some doubts lingered.

"I need to hit the putting green," Jack murmured, glancing at Matt. His fingers fumbled with the zipper on his bag as he took out his putter and a few golf balls.

He walked toward the putting green, his shoes leaving a trail in the dew-soaked grass. The green stretched out before him, alive with competitors absorbed in practice, their sharp focus revealing just how much was at stake.

A chill ran up his spine, alerting him someone was watching. Even without looking, Jack sensed Nick's stare cutting through the crowd.

Sure enough, just as Jack reached the fringe, they locked eyes for a moment before Jack looked away and kept walking, acting like he meant to head to the far side of the green all along.

Reaching his practice spot, Jack spied Nick sinking a long putt with ease. Nick smirked and fist-pumped as he walked toward the hole. As he picked up his ball, Nick shot Jack a confident glance, as if sure he'd beat Jack again.

Jack clenched his jaw, heat rising in his chest. He wasn't just playing for a win—he was playing to take Nick down.

As he adjusted his glove, Jack overheard a coach's hushed advice to another player: "Focus on your tempo, trust your swing, commit to the shot, and play the course one shot at a time." Jack nodded, absorbing the advice as though it were meant for him.

Why can't I have some simple keys like that? Jack wondered as he dropped three golf balls onto the green. His thoughts flashed to his coach, Taylor, a young assistant pro who focused solely on the player's swing.

Jack chewed his lip, his stomach knotting. *What if I lose my swing? What if everything falls apart again?* Each question heightened his sense of impending doom.

Jack rolled his shoulders and lined up for his first putt. As he swung his putter, the familiar rhythm of his practice stroke soothed his jittery nerves. His hands stayed steady, though his stomach churned. He took a deep breath, blocking out the crowd's murmurs and Nick's looming presence. The putt rolled smoothly across the green, curving just at the right moment to drop into the hole.

Jack's shoulders relaxed, a grin tugging at the corner of his mouth. Confidence began to replace the tight knot in his chest. Jack lined up another putt, a bit longer this time. He felt comfortable over the putts, feeling an easy rhythm with each practice swing.

One by one, the balls rolled into or near the hole. With each successful putt, the tension lessened in his muscles, and a small, proud smile appeared. Thoughts of Nick faded from Jack's mind. He gathered his golf balls and walked back toward the clubhouse. His steps were lighter, and he felt ready to go.

Matt, who had been watching, came over with a big, encouraging smile. He gave Jack a fist bump. "See? It's just like any other day on the course. You can do this, Jack."

Jack flashed a quick smile at Matt, grateful for his constant support. "Thanks, Matt."

"Keep it going. You've got the putter on fire—everyone's going to notice."

"Let's go see who I'm playing with," Jack said, motioning toward the clubhouse.

They stepped into the building, where the buzz of pre-tournament chatter filled the air, mixing with the aroma of freshly brewed coffee.

Framed photos of past champions lined the walls, their serious faces staring down at Jack as if challenging him to join them. His eyes locked on a familiar face—last year's champion, Nick.

Oh, look, there's that smug look of his. I just want to wipe that smirk off his face! Jack thought. A jolt of energy surged through him, reigniting his fierce determination to prevent history from repeating itself.

Jack and Matt made their way to the crowded notice board, with the surrounding chatter amplifying Jack's growing anxiety. Scanning the list of pairings, Jack's stomach tightened. His finger traced down the names until it landed on his own, and right beside it, in bold letters, was "Nick Sanders." His heart skipped a beat.

"Looks like it's you and Nick," Matt said, peering over Jack's shoulder. "That's going to be one intense match." His excitement barely masked his concern.

Jack's throat tightened, his voice barely escaping as a whisper. "Matt, this… is going to be tough," he said, trying to muster confidence.

"Hey, just play the course, not Nick," Matt said, aiming to lift Jack's spirits. "Stick to what you know, trust your swing, and you'll be fine."

"Thanks, Matt," Jack replied, his nerves steadying as determination took over. "I'm ready to leave it all on the course," Jack said, a spark of determination lighting his eyes. "This could be the day everything changes."

Strengthen Your Game

1. How do you prepare for an important round to ensure you're fully ready?

2. What distractions do you face before a round, and how do you plan to handle them?

3. How do you currently manage pre-round anxiety, and what changes might help you stay calmer?

CHAPTER 2

A Tale of Two Nines

Jack's tee time was rapidly approaching as he reached the first tee. Nick was already there, his swings smooth and perfect, making it look easy.

Nick paused, his eyes narrowing as they met Jack's. "Sullivan, it's just you and me," he said with a smirk, his voice oozing sarcasm. "Big day, huh? Ready to show us what you've got?"

Jack adjusted his cap, his usual move when he was nervous. "As ready as ever," he said, trying to sound confident.

"Bet you remember last year. You only beat me because I pulled a muscle in my back. I could barely swing. After that, I won every match."

Nick took a slow practice swing. "Every time you'd get the lead, and, well, you remember."

Jack's stomach twisted at Nick's words. He kept his face calm, but his thoughts churned. *Seriously? Did I win just because he was hurt? Was it just luck?*

Jack took a deep breath and fidgeted with the clubs in his bag. "Yeah, I remember," he said, trying to sound casual. But his heart pounded, and doubt gnawed at him.

The crackle of the announcer's voice cut through the air. "Next on the tee, from Westview High, Jack Sullivan."

Jack's heart thumped louder.

This was his big moment. Light applause rippled through the crowd. Jack's sandy hair peeked out from under his cap as he tried to hide his nerves behind a focused stare. He glanced at Matt, who nodded, letting him know he had his back.

Jack teed his ball, his grip solid on the driver. His eyes scanned the shadowy fairway ahead. In his mind, Jack traced the perfect arc of his drive. He'd played Willow Springs so many times, he knew every hole and every hazard like the back of his hand. Hole number one was a par four with water on the right and a big sand trap on the left.

Jack inhaled deeply, waggled his club, and swung. The sharp crack of the club hitting the ball echoed a perfect shot. His ball soared, landing in the middle of the fairway, a full 280 yards out. A proud smile crept onto his face as the crowd applauded.

Off to a good start. A moment of pride fluttered inside him.

Nick's tee shot was a laser, landing just before Jack's but bounding past, as if a silent taunt. Nick's smug grin tugged at Jack, but he looked away, focusing on his own game.

Jack's drive set him up perfectly for his second shot. The pin was in the back center of the green. Watching the flag flutter in the cool morning breeze, Jack pulled out his 9-iron without a second thought.

Swing feels good. I'm swinging it pure, Jack reminded himself, taking a few practice swings to get the perfect rhythm.

His shot sailed gracefully into the clear sky. Almost as if in slow-motion, it landed softly on the green and rolled within three feet of the pin. Jack walked to the green, confident he would make his putt.

After Nick two-putted for par, it was Jack's turn. He crouched, reading the green like a detective. He lined up and rolled the ball smoothly into the cup for birdie.

One under, he thought, feeling a surge of confidence.

Jack's game flowed—four pars on the next four holes. His confidence grew with each shot. Nick kept pace with pars of his own.

The sixth was a long par five, a great chance for Jack to get his birdie. His drive was powerful, the ball screaming through the air. It was his longest drive of the day.

"Whoa! Where'd that come from?" Nick chirped.

Jack ignored Nick and slid his driver into his bag. A quick glance at Matt earned him a fist-pump and nod.

Determined, Jack grabbed his 5-wood, aiming boldly for the green. The ball fell just short, but a perfect pitch left him four feet from the cup. With a smooth stroke, he sank the putt for a well-earned birdie.

Two under through six, Jack thought. *Keep this up and we could win this thing.*

Nick matched Jack's birdie. Walking to the next tee, Nick sneered, "Lucky today, huh, Sullivan? But you know how luck is—it doesn't last."

Jack shrugged off Nick's words and filled in his scorecard.

Relaxed, Jack's swing was smooth and effortless. His mind was quiet. Unaware of Nick and the crowd, it felt like he was the only person on the course. Jack was in complete control. He was in the zone.

On the seventh hole, a par three, his tee shot found the trap guarding the front of the green. Calmly, he grabbed his sand wedge and, like a skilled surgeon, went to work. His bunker shot was perfect. Sand sprayed into the air, and the ball stopped just inches from the hole.

"Way to go!" he whispered, feeling the rush after saving par.

He and Nick made par on the eighth, Jack sinking a tricky fifteen-foot putt.

The ninth hole was tough, one of the most challenging on the course, with bunkers on the fairway and around the green. Jack secured a par, but Nick missed a long par putt and settled for a bogey.

The first nine holes were a blur of great shots and well-judged putts. Jack was playing the best golf of his life, tied for the lead and two strokes ahead of Nick.

Jack stared at the leaderboard, realizing just how well he'd played. *I don't know how that happened. It just did.*

A sudden thought struck him: *What if I blow this?* His knees wobbled under the weight of the pressure.

Nick strolled past him, giving a condescending glance. "Nice front nine, Sullivan. It's always like that for you, huh? A good front nine and then, well, you know. The real match starts now."

A surge of irritation flowed through Jack. *I can't let Nick get into my head.*

However, something had shifted. Jack was more aware of Nick than at any other time in the round.

"I'm playing the best golf of my life, and he's only a few shots behind me. I can't make any mistakes. I just can't let this one slip away," he whispered.

The tenth fairway suddenly seemed narrower, the hazards scarier. Jack's stomach tightened as he scanned the crowd, noticing the college coaches' eyes on him for the first time.

This is my big break. I can't mess this up. Jack scrunched his forehead.

Doubt flickered within Jack again. *Nick's sure he's going to beat me.* Jack rubbed the side of his face. *He's playing well. Somehow, I gotta hold him off.*

Jack tried to find the calm he had on the front nine, but the doubts were dug in, refusing to budge. He fidgeted with his cap and placed his ball on the tee, aware of his tightened jaw and grip.

Beat Nick! I gotta beat Nick, replayed in his head.

His drive on the tenth hole veered right, landing in the thick rough. Jack sighed deeply, pressing his lips together as a lump formed in his throat.

Nick crushed his drive, sending the ball hurtling down the fairway. He smirked and nodded at Jack.

Jack hurried to his second shot and snatched a club from his bag, almost pretending that the last shot didn't happen.

As he lined up his second shot, his mind whirled with negative thoughts. His swing was rushed, and the ball buried itself in a sand trap guarding the left front of the green.

Thud!

His club struck the sand with force, barely moving the golf ball. His doubts turned to panic. After barely escaping the bunker on his next effort, Jack faced a long downhill putt on the rippling green. Meanwhile, Nick's ball sat inside three feet from the cup.

He wiped his sweaty palms on his pants, lined up the putt, and backed away. The hole looked so small; the break confusing. Rushed and still uneasy, he struck the ball.

"Stop! Stop!" Jack commanded.

His disobedient ball kept rolling, stopping seven feet past the hole. He missed another putt before finally finding the cup for a triple bogey. Nick made birdie. Just like that, Jack's lead vanished.

"Tough one, Sullivan. That's how it goes sometimes. You're playing great, and then suddenly you lose it," Nick said, faking empathy.

Jack nodded and jammed his putter into his bag, noticing Matt's frown in the crowd.

Tension filled his body. *I blew it! Why can't I get it together? I'm terrible!*

Nick parred the next three holes as Jack went bogey, bogey, par.

Jack's drive on the par five fourteen found the middle of the fairway. Nick's drive outpaced him by twenty-five yards. To Jack, the lake between them and the pin stretched like an ocean. He faced a tough decision: go for the green in two—a risky shot that could pay off big—or play it safe and lay up.

I've got to go for it. Nick will get on in two from where he's at. I'm just going to have to really crush it, he thought before taking an aggressive swing. It came out low and thin.

Plop!

The ball hit the water, the sound marking a failed gamble.

Jack's heart sank along with his ball. "I should have played it safe. Why did I take that risk?" he muttered, smacking his club on the ground.

Nick shrugged, a glint in his eye.

Jack had made a critical mistake. He played his opponent instead of playing the course.

After a series of disastrous putts, Jack recorded another triple bogey on his card. Nick's second shot soared over the lake and landed perfectly on the green, twelve feet from the cup. It was a two-putt from there for his birdie. The zone Jack was in during the front nine was gone, just like his chances of winning.

As the round continued, Jack's shots grew less precise, his errors more glaring. The once-fluid swing was tense and awkward. He over thought every swing, second-guessed every decision. It was almost as if he'd never played before.

Nick, meanwhile, was playing confidently and now led the tournament.

On the eighteenth hole, Jack's two-foot putt spun around the edge of the cup before mercifully dropping in. The sting of defeat was raw. The murmurs of the crowd were a distant buzz, his negative self-talk louder. *I blew it. I had a shot to beat Nick. I fell apart again. I just want to get out of here.*

Jack forced a smile as he shook Nick's hand. "Good job," he said, his voice heavy with disappointment.

"Thanks. I was feeling it today. I was sure I was going to win this thing. Another rough one for you, huh?"

Before Jack could reply, Nick's eyes shifted to the crowd, and he jogged off the green, leaving Jack to his own thoughts.

Jack played the best golf of his life on the front nine. The back nine was another story. His mental game unraveled, taking his physical game with it. He went from tied for the lead to finishing a crushing twenty-fifth after a forty-five on the back nine.

Matt walked over, hoisting Jack's bag. "It's okay, Jack. You had some great shots out there. You'll beat him next time."

Jack nodded, but he knew he had a lot to learn about tournament golf. He had played two very different nines today, and he knew which one he wanted to play next time.

Strengthen Your Game

1. When you lose focus or struggle during a round, what usually throws you off?

2. What do you do to refocus and recover when your game starts to slip?

3. How challenging is it for you to stay focused on only the next shot, and what makes it difficult?

CHAPTER 3

The Old Pro's Secret

Jack dragged his feet toward the car, the clattering of his golf clubs echoing his frustration after the round he'd just blown. His dad leaned silently against the car, just like after every rough round. Jack's eyes darted between the ground and his dad, his face tightening with a blend of anger and defeat. He tossed his bag into the trunk a little harder than necessary, the metallic echo ringing out like a harsh reminder of his failure.

As the car hummed along the highway, Jack stared out the window, every missed shot swirling in his mind. His thoughts ricocheted between the thrill of the front nine and the bitter collapse of the back. He thought about every lesson, every dollar his dad poured into his game—money that didn't come easy. The weight of it pressed down on him like a debt he'd never repay. The silence grew heavier with every passing mile.

Jack's dad finally broke the silence, his voice soft but probing. "You were on fire during the front nine, leading the pack. Must've felt awesome, huh?"

Jack spoke slowly, his voice barely above a whisper. "The front nine is always easier. Less pressure. But then… I fell apart. Just like I always do." His words hung in the air.

His dad nodded, expecting the conversation to end there.

But Jack wasn't done. His thoughts spilled out. "I just don't get it. I practice so hard, my swing feels good, but when it counts, I choke. It's like I'm cursed or something. Coaches won't want a player who falls apart when it matters."

Jack's voice rose, a mix of anger and helplessness as he turned to face his dad. "I need a scholarship for college, Dad. But who wants a choker? I see my swing flaws on video, and I can fix them. But how do you fix choking? How do you fix messing up the easiest shots when everyone's watching?"

As Jack's frustration poured out, his dad quietly pulled the car over to the side of the road. His dad turned toward Jack with a concerned look twisting on his face. "Jack, you're too tough on yourself," his dad said with a concerned look.

"You're an amazing player. Don't let these few rough rounds make you hate what you love. I'm not much of a golfer, but it's clear how these tournaments throw you off. It's painful for your mom and me to watch you like this. But I think you need to look at the game differently. You hit some amazing shots that most people could only dream of hitting. I don't think you give yourself a chance to let those amazing talents happen enough in tournaments."

Jack gazed at his dad, waiting for the answer that all kids expect their parents to have. Jack suddenly felt like he was eight again. As a teenager, it was the first time in a while he needed his dad to solve a problem.

In a small voice, Jack asked, "What should I do, Dad? This is killing me. I don't even know if I want to play in tournaments anymore. I put all this work in on the range for nothing, it seems."

"Remember how good your uncle John was in tournaments? He's the one who got you into golf, right? He spent hours with Charlie Jones, the old golf pro who still hangs around Jamesville Municipal. Your uncle said Mr. Jones didn't just fix his swing, but taught him how to handle the pressure of competitive golf."

His dad told him more about Mr. Jones, a former pro with an outstanding college career and countless mini-tour wins. He was on track for the PGA Tour until a freak shoulder injury cut his career short. For years, Mr. Jones was bitter about losing his passion—a passion passed down from his dad, a PGA professional who learned from a former Tour player from the fifties. Now, though, Mr. Jones loved talking golf and had plenty of strong opinions about the game. People still remembered his playing days, and when he talked, they listened.

He was a tough character who was generous with his time for those who listened and learned from his wisdom.

"So, Jack, I think he's the one you should talk to," Mr. Sullivan said.

Jack had seen Mr. Jones around the clubhouse, but had never worked up the courage to talk to him.

But now, coming off his loss against Nick yet again, Jack said, "Dad, I'm willing to try anything."

* * *

Two days later, Jack pulled up to Jamesville Municipal with a swirl of nerves and excitement. Those feelings continued with every jittery step as he walked into the building. The old pro sat alone at a table, scribbling notes on a scrap of paper. Jack hesitated, then slowly made his way over, unsure of what to say. Mr. Jones glanced up, his eyebrows raised in curiosity.

"Hi, Mr. Jones. I'm Jack... Jack Sullivan," Jack said with all the confidence he could muster.

"Call me Charlie. Mr. Jones was my dad," the old pro said, flashing a quick smile. "Sullivan. Sure, Jack Sullivan. Your uncle John talks about you and I was hoping we'd meet one day. So, what brings you by?"

Jack knew it was time for honesty. "I choke under pressure in tournaments, and I need help. I just played in the Grand Strand Tournament. I was leading after the front nine, but the back nine... it all fell apart. One thing went wrong, then everything spiraled out of control."

Charlie's gray eyes were intimidating, but a hint of kindness softened them. He knew Jack came from a wonderful family and, more importantly, really needed help. Jack looked ready to try something different.

"I've heard about your game. People say you've got a great swing, real talent. So, you're already partway down the road to success. What was it like when you were playing the first nine?" Charlie asked, taking a slow sip of his coffee.

A slow grin crept across Jack's face. "Everything just clicked. My swing felt so smooth, like I didn't even have to think about it. My mind went completely quiet—no doubts, no worrying about who I was up against or who was watching. It was just me and the course, and suddenly, golf felt... simple."

"So, what about the back nine?" Charlie asked, raising an eyebrow.

Jack sighed; his grin faded. "As soon as I started doubting myself, everything felt wrong. My swing was off, like I was fighting my own body. My mind wouldn't stop second-guessing every swing. I thought too much about the other guy, the crowd, and especially my score. Every bad shot made me panic more. Golf felt impossible."

Jack rubbed his face. "I don't know what happened to my swing. It just fell apart all of a sudden."

Charlie leaned in, raising his eyebrows. "We need to work on something else—your mind. I bet you've never thought much about the mental side of golf, right? It's way more important than you think."

Jack paused, considering Charlie's words. "Yeah, I've heard about the mental game, but never really looked into it. I always thought if I just practiced my swing hard enough, my scores would get better. That's all Taylor, my swing coach, and I work on. It seems like my confidence is based on how I'm swinging. When I'm swinging well, I'm confident, but it just takes one bad shot, and the confidence disappears."

Charlie gave a small smile. "When confidence is based only on your swing, you're always one bad shot away from losing it. That's why the mental game is just as important as your swing. It's challenging to learn, but once you do, tournaments will be a lot more fun. You'll feel more in control. From what your dad told me, you want to play college golf. If you can control yourself better, you'll have an edge over the competition, and you will stand out to college coaches."

Jack often watched college events on the Golf Channel, noticing a few players who looked, scored, and acted like seasoned pros. He assumed they were simply physically better than the other players. But now, he realized there was more to it than just physical skill. These players had a great mental game. They stayed in control no matter what and focused on each shot. They aimed to win the next shot, nothing more. Jack knew he needed to learn the secret of doing the same thing.

Strengthen Your Game

1. Who do you trust to talk about your game, and what qualities make them a good sounding board?

2. What is the best piece of advice you've received about your golf game, and how has it helped you?

3. How open are you to seeking advice and hearing different perspectives on your game?

CHAPTER 4

The Routine: A Golfer's Secret Weapon

After just a few minutes with Charlie, a flicker of hope ignited in Jack's heart. It was as if a door had opened, giving him a new way to see his struggles—and now he was eager for more. Jack trusted Charlie, feeling a quiet confidence growing inside him. Maybe Charlie's approach could be the key to turning his tournament play around.

Charlie leaned in. "Jack, let me ask you something. Have you ever nailed a 300-yard drive right down the fairway? Or hit a 5-iron inside ten feet? Gotten a tough chip close or drained a fifteen-foot putt? I'm guessing the answer is yes. That tells me you've got the skill, so why can't you do it consistently in tournaments?"

Jack thought for a moment. "Sometimes it just flows. No bad thoughts. I feel confident in my swing. I pick the target and let it fly."

Charlie's eyes lit up. "That's exactly where we want to be in tournaments! But it's tougher when the pressure's on, right? When you're up against serious competition? Every mistake feels like a step backward. But here's where we start: a new productive pre-shot routine. It's the foundation of a stronger mental game. Your routine helps you treat every shot the same.

It'll help focus your mind, which relaxes the body, giving you the best chance to play your best golf, especially in tournaments where there are so many distractions."

Charlie took a sip of his coffee. "Tell me, do you have a routine?"

"I take some practice swings, set up, glance at the target, waggle the club a bit, then swing," Jack said. "I sort of just do what the pros do and try to copy that."

"That's a start, but it's just the physical part. What's going through your mind during those practice swings?" Charlie asked, tapping the side of his head.

"I guess it's never the same thing. It seems like when I'm not playing well, I'm thinking about a lot of stuff. It's stuff like my bad shots on the last hole, my score, or even what people are thinking of me. If I'm playing well, I guess I'm not thinking about anything right before the shot. I just play."

Charlie leaned in. "Well, there's something you probably don't know. The PGA Tour pros don't just have a physical routine; they have a solid mental routine. A great routine puts the focus where it needs to be on this next shot. It helps you commit to the best choice, picture the shot, and remind yourself what you need to do with your swing. It sets up your body and connects you to the target, so you can swing freely."

"So, it's sorta like I only have half a routine. Mine is all physical. No wonder my mind is everywhere but where it needs to be," Jack said, shoulders slumping, his eyes on his lap. With a heavy sigh, he forced himself to meet Charlie's steady gaze.

Charlie flashed an encouraging smile. "A solid routine is the foundation for a more consistent swing. It'll engage your mind and help you focus, giving your body the best chance of executing the great swing you've practiced. It'll help you with pressure in tournaments—distractions like your score, your position, bad shots, tough holes, bad breaks, even unfriendly playing partners, and more. Those distractions are always competing for your attention when you're trying to hit a shot."

Jack nodded. "I've got to admit, my mind's always worrying about something—my swing, my score, or an awful hole. No wonder I can't focus on every shot. Those distractions are exactly what I'm aware of every time I play in tournaments. When I'm playing for fun, they're not there. I'm just trying to hit good shots, and if I mess up, it doesn't really matter. I just play the next shot without overthinking everything."

Charlie offered another smile and clapped once. "Here's why the routine works. If your mind is locked into the routine, those distractions lose their grip. It's like a protective force field around you. The distractions are still out there, but they can't get inside because your mind is busy with positive, focused thoughts."

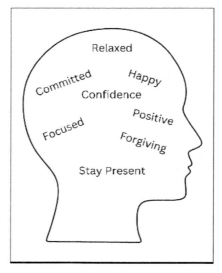

No pressure - golf is fun and easy.

The distractions of tournament play make playing your best much harder.

Strengthen Your Game

1. How often do you approach a shot without a clear plan, and how does that impact your game?

2. Do you have a pre-shot routine that you use consistently?

3. Why is having a consistent, effective routine important for your confidence and performance?

CHAPTER 5

What You Do Between Shots Matters

"Golf is a game of shots and breaks in the action. It's what you do between shots that is one key to playing your best. We can build a great routine, but if you sabotage yourself in between shots, it's going to be really difficult to hit a successful shot."

"What do you mean by sabotaging myself?" Jack asked, a puzzled look crossing his face.

"Go back to that last tournament, where you had the great front nine. What was it like between shots?"

"I couldn't wait to hit the next shot. I was confident in my swing; I was relaxed, and I was enjoying the experience of playing great in a tournament. One thing that stood out was how I walked and talked with confidence—nothing really bothered me, even if I hit it out of position."

"What a great feeling! Golf is easy when you feel like that, isn't it? Everything flows, your rhythm is great, and you're happy and in control. Do you see how that leads to being in a good frame of mind to hit great shots, even in a tournament round? Your mind, body, and emotions were free, weren't they? So what changed on the back nine?"

Jack furrowed his brow as the tournament replayed through his mind. "I've been going over that in my head ever since. I remember walking off the ninth green, and there was a leaderboard that I looked at. I saw my name at the top of it, and Nick said something that made me mad and threw me off. Suddenly, I felt different. It was a mixture of nerves, anger at Nick because I knew he was trying to get in my head, tightness—I walked quicker, didn't want to talk to anyone—and that was before I even got to the tenth tee. I hit a terrible drive, and it spiraled from there."

"Do you see how in that time between the putt on nine and the drive on ten, your mindset and emotions changed and made it almost impossible to focus and make that free swing on ten, that you had achieved for almost all the front nine? What else do you remember from that back nine?"

"I must admit, it all happened so quickly. I don't remember much of anything. It's a bit like I don't want to remember anything because it was so disappointing." Jack sighed.

"That's very normal; awareness is such a big part of it. Take a moment and see if anything springs to mind." Charlie's voice was encouraging.

Jack took a few seconds, then answered, "I guess I really started thinking about my score and the 'what ifs'—both good and bad. 'What if I birdie the easy par five in a couple of holes? I can get a shot back. What if I miss this short putt? What if I hit this risky shot and save par?' I couldn't commit to a number of shots. I knew it was the wrong choice or the wrong club, but I still hit it. On the front nine, I was talking with my best friend Matt as he was following me. We talked about school, his girlfriend, and how much I was enjoying the day. On the back nine, I kind of avoided him because I was embarrassed at how I was playing. The only thing I said to him after I chunked a chip and then three-putted was how much I suck and that I have no business playing in tournaments after he tried to encourage me."

No judgment rested in Charlie's eyes as he said, "Let me ask you a question. Let's say that Matt was caddying for you, and he told you during your round how much you suck and how you have no business playing in tournaments. What would your reaction be?"

Jack chuckled, trying to imagine the absurd scene. "Pretty sure that even though he's my best friend, I would've fired him on the spot. Maybe even decked him."

"So would I!" Charlie gave a hearty chuckle. "So, why would you tell yourself those things? Do you see now how what you do, and how you talk to yourself between shots, affects how easy it is to hit good shots consistently, especially under the pressure of tournament play?"

Jack sat there, Charlie's words sinking in. It was like a light had turned on in a dark room. "Wow, I never thought of it like that."

Charlie chuckled again. "Totally understandable. So, if we can consciously have productive thoughts and actions between shots, implement a focused, productive routine before the shot, and react as positively as possible no matter what happens, we can give ourselves the best chance of winning the next shot way more often and make scoring under pressure way easier. Let's go to the course and start focusing on these steps and see if we can help you rethink how you approach the game. What do you say?"

Jack sat there for a moment, taking in everything Charlie had talked about for the last thirty minutes. Something special was stirring inside him. It was a plan where no plan had existed before. His mind drifted to picturing the success that he wanted so badly because he now believed that this was the moment where everything was about to change.

Jack shot to his feet. "Charlie, I'm ready. I can't wait to get started—let's go!"

Strengthen Your Game

1. How often does your mind dwell on the last shot instead of focusing on the current one?

2. Think back to your last great round. What were your thoughts between shots? Compare that with your between shots thinking during a poor round.

3. As you move from one shot to the next, how aware are you of your thoughts and body language?

CHAPTER 6

The Building Blocks of Success

Jack and Charlie walked to the range, Jack eager and full of hope. His time with Charlie left him with a sense of assurance and trust. He trusted him not only because of his experience and success as a player, but also because of the thoughtful questions he asked and the answers he gave. Jack couldn't wait to hear what Charlie would say next.

"Let's see you hit a few 7-irons, Jack. Don't worry about where they go, just swing."

Smack!

With no warm-up, Jack launched a perfect fade.

"Do it again."

Thump!

Another one soared into the sky and landed very close to the flag 160 yards away.

"You hit it better than I'd heard!" Charlie exclaimed with a smile. "No warm-up, you just aimed and fired at the target. So why don't you do that every time?"

Jack looked at Charlie. "I do that a lot in practice and when it doesn't mean much, but when I get in a tournament, it doesn't feel nearly as smooth and free."

Charlie smiled. "Let's build you the winning routine that we talked about in the clubhouse. That will help you be more focused on the simple task of winning the next shot. It all starts with committing to a shot that you KNOW you can hit, not one you THINK you can hit. That knowledge comes from how you practice. If you practice with a 7-iron and hit the same full shot with a fade, that is what you should hit on the course. If you don't successfully practice different shots and different shapes over and over, you shouldn't try them in tournaments. Do you see how it's easier to fully commit to a shot you know you can hit?"

"That's interesting. I often hit shots in tournaments that I never really practice, and now that I think about it, most of the time they don't come off, and I end up getting mad when I put myself in a tough position. I see the best players hit different shapes, spins, and trajectories, and I think I need to copy them to be successful."

"Have you ever asked those players how they practice?" Charlie asked.

"No, I just thought they were really good."

"That's the first lesson of being fully committed: Only hit the shots on the course that you practice with success. That will help you commit to the best option. Now we have the shot we know we can hit. The target isn't always the flag when you hit to the green. Most greens are twenty-five to forty yards deep. If you divide the green into two halves, you will be able to hit a full shorter club somewhere in that front half and a full longer club to the back half. Match the full shot to which half of the green the flag is in. So now we have a comfortable shot we can commit to. You don't have to hit every approach shot pin high to score well."

Charlie's eyebrows lifted, "Now, what happens if the flag is in a tough position for your fade?"

"I really struggle with any flag on the left side of the green. To hit my fade, I feel like I've got to aim at the left edge of the green to get it close, which means I'm looking at bunkers, water, or tough short sides if it doesn't fade. Most of the time, I steer away at the last minute because I'm afraid of missing it in those bad spots. Sometimes I miss the green way right, but sometimes I feel anxious, get quick and pull it left." Jack sighed, remembering times he had messed that up.

"Would it be easier to make a full, free swing to a spot right in the middle of the green and try to make a twenty-five-footer? Do you think you could make a more committed, aggressive swing if you weren't looking at trouble as you stood over the ball?"

"Yes, but all the best players seem to hit it close to wherever the flag is on the green."

"Jack, those guys practice a variety of shots over and over again until they can confidently bring that into tournament play. That may take months and months to be ready to do that. Right now, you have a big tournament coming up, and we need to keep it as simple and stress-free as possible. You will still make birdies, but you will make fewer mistakes and, as a result, fewer bogeys. We absolutely want to change our practice habits, but right now we need to commit to hitting shots we know we can hit confidently. Does that sound like a game plan for making full commitment a habit?" Charlie offered with an encouraging smile.

"Yes, sir, I see exactly what you're talking about. That makes a lot of sense because I make enough birdies to be successful, but make too many soft bogeys that turn a good round into a disappointing round. What's the next step?"

"For you, based on our game plan, it's to clearly visualize your shot—that strong fade that starts left of the target and moves to the target. Your swing is built for that shot, and if you're committed, it should be very repeatable. Look at that blue flag out there about 160 yards away—that's our ultimate target. What I want you to visualize is where the ball will start, how high it will fly, and really see that ball move back to the blue flag. Now describe how you see what the ball needs to do."

"Okay, I want to see it start on the left edge of the practice green where the blue flag is, about ten yards left of the flag, rise in the air about thirty feet above the trees in the background, and then fade towards the flag."

"Amazing visualization, Jack. Do you sense how engaged your mind is to picture that shot? It's tougher to do under the pressure of competition, but the more you practice it, the easier it will become."

"I can feel my imagination being much stronger and my mind clearer. What's next?" Jack couldn't keep the eagerness out of his voice.

"I know you've had lessons, and you have a fantastic swing, but do you know what it is in your swing that, if you achieve it, you'll probably hit a good shot? And if you forget to do it, chances are it won't be too good?"

Jack always felt like he clearly understood his swing, so he could answer confidently. "There are two things that I've narrowed down by looking at it on video and talking to Taylor, the pro who helps me with my swing. I tend to roll the club inside on the way back, so I need to feel like the club stays outside my hands halfway back. And I sometimes get quick from the top, especially when I'm nervous, and it throws my timing off. I really struggle with that piece in tournaments when I get tight and nervous. I really like to copy Hideki Matsuyama from the top of the backswing and try to feel a really nice, full follow-through and balanced finish like Rory McIlroy. If I can do those things, I usually hit a good shot."

"They are perfect models, Jack, so how about we incorporate those feelings and imitations into your practice swing, along with a practice waggle, like Justin Thomas, to make sure the club doesn't roll inside? See how intentional that practice swing has become now? Remember how you said you just used to do a practice swing because you watched the pros on TV do it? In effect, it's like a freebie real swing without hitting the ball, but now that intention is right at the forefront of your mind before you hit the shot for real."

"I see how much more purpose these steps have. It really helps me to understand much more clearly what it means to be engaged mentally. Usually, my mind kind of wanders, or it's still thinking about something that happened before. Now it's more in the present. I hear the pros talk about being in the present when they get interviewed, and I didn't really understand what they meant—now I do!" His eyes lit up.

"You're a quick learner, Jack!" Charlie clapped. "So, we've committed to a shot you know you can hit, imagined it clearly, and felt your keys to success in your practice swing. Now we need to learn to get set up consistently to the ball, connect to the target, and then just let it go. This part seems easy, but lots of people do everything right and then ruin it with a poor setup and alignment."

Strengthen Your Game

1. How often do you attempt a shot that you're not sure you can pull off?

2. Do you find yourself taking risks with approach shots, and are those choices based on emotion or strategy?

3. What do you consider the key elements that make your swing successful?

4. Could you dedicate a focused fifteen seconds to fully engage in your routine before every swing?

CHAPTER 7

Set Up and Let It Go!

"So, Jack, we've done all the hard work learning about the routine, but all of that work can be undone by not setting up to the ball correctly and consistently. So many players struggle to align to the target, and it's usually a couple of reasons that make what seems like a simple task difficult. How confident are you that you align well?"

"I feel pretty sure I do because I practice with an alignment rod on the ground, so I figure if I do it enough, that will guarantee good alignment." Jack nodded.

"Most top junior players do that, and it usually works on the golf course, but sometimes it becomes inconsistent without the rod on the ground, especially if they don't practice without that aid. It's something you have to practice intentionally, so it translates to the golf course," Charlie cautioned.

"You know what, I sometimes feel awkward at address where things don't look or feel right, and it makes me uncomfortable, especially in tournaments. I feel like I steer the ball instead of just letting it go and releasing it."

"It's tough to make a confident, committed swing when you're uncomfortable, isn't it, Jack?"

"Yes, it is. I see where I'd have to manipulate the swing or the clubface a bit to counteract poor aim. So how do I set up more efficiently?"

Charlie clapped once and shifted his weight from one foot to the other. "Let's recap our routine. You've committed to a shot you know you can hit; you've visualized what it's going to do, and you've felt what your swing needs to do to be successful. Now you want to take a breath and relax. Walk into the ball, and set the clubface behind it, pointed at an intermediate target about five yards in front of the ball in line with the final target."

"It may be a divot, weed, leaf, or something else that's in line with the target. Once that clubface is set, move your feet to be parallel to that line—maybe just open your stance a little to help your fade. Now you're set up nicely. Trust that nothing is going to change and shift your focus to the target. Do that pre-shot waggle we talked about to help prevent the club from rolling inside. Now, connect fully to the target for two or three seconds, move your eyes back to the ball and settle, then let it go with good rhythm, balance, tempo, and freedom."

"Accept the results, whatever happens. What we've done is allow you to focus on everything that you have control over. It doesn't guarantee a great shot, but it makes it more likely, and whatever happens, you can react with no regrets because you did everything you could do that was under your control. That is the essence of your routine—productive steps and no regrets after no 'what ifs' that you wish you could do over again. If you can commit to this process, your tournament play will be MUCH better, and you will enjoy competitive play much more."

Charlie's face looked serious. "Let me ask you how many shots on the back nine of the tournament that, for one reason or another, you wish you could have had a mulligan?"

"Almost all of them," Jack said.

Charlie leaned in. "Our goal is to have no regrets."

"So when can I start hitting shots with this routine?" Jack asked eagerly.

"Now is as good a time as any. Let's get to work!" Charlie gave a thumbs-up.

Strengthen Your Game

1. How often do you feel uncomfortable over the ball without knowing the reason?

2. Has a coach or teammate ever mentioned that your alignment needs work? How did you respond?

3. If you trust your routine and preparation, could it help you swing freer and steer it less?

CHAPTER 8

Focused Practice Makes the Game Routine

It was a very different feeling for Jack to have to think consciously about what to do. Charlie handed him a 7-iron. "Let's hit it at that red flag. Based on what we've talked about, what's your plan?"

"I'm going to hit this full 7-iron at the red flag. The ball will start about five yards left of it, fly at medium height, and fade to the target."

"That's a great plan, Jack. What comes next?"

"Well, I've committed to a shot I know I can hit. I've visualized the flight, and now I'm going to take a practice swing with a waggle to help me keep the club on the correct path. Then I'll feel that really nice transition, like Hideki Matsuyama."

Jack made the waggle and exaggerated not rushing from the top. His club hit the perfect low point just past where the ball would be. It gave him confidence because the swing felt so good. He couldn't wait to hit the shot.

"Would you mind if I talk you through the next steps, and you follow my directions?" Charlie asked.

"That sounds good to me," Jack replied.

"Okay, Jack, you've done everything right. Pick a spot between you and the target. You see that sandy divot about five yards in front of the ball? It's right in line with the flag. Walk in and focus on setting that clubface aimed at that divot."

Jack slowly approached the ball, keeping his attention on the divot. He set the club down perfectly straight at it.

"Now set your feet parallel to that target line. That looks great. Don't worry anymore about that now. Get your focus on the red flag and picture the ball starting five yards left of it."

"That's a different look for me because I'm not focusing on the ball like I used to."

"Fall in love with that target. Take a nice, settling breath to calm you, just like a target shooter does before they fire. Now slowly bring your eyes back to the ball, settle again, and react to the target. Let it go!"

Jack swung. The ball soared into the air, starting a little farther left than he wanted, but it faded back, landing about twenty-five feet from the target. Jack was disappointed and told Charlie he had pulled it.

Charlie's eyes lit up. "That was a really well-struck shot. Amazingly enough, twenty-five feet is the average proximity to the hole from 150 yards on the PGA Tour."

"Wow, I thought they'd hit that shot a lot closer. I'm right there with them." Jack smiled.

"How would you grade your routine and execution?" Charlie asked.

Jack squinted. "Everything before I swung felt great, but if I'm being honest, the swing felt a little quick from the top."

"Awesome awareness, Jack. It was a little quick. Doesn't it feel less stressful when we don't worry too much about the mechanics of the swing and focus more on the feel of it as a whole? For your next shot, I want you to focus a little more on that transition from the top in the practice swing. When you're looking at the target, remind yourself to let it set at the top. One more thing—you don't need to be perfect. With a productive routine, even when it's not perfect, it's still very playable. Now, hit this next shot without me saying anything."

Jack went through his routine, and this time, he hit it perfectly—just like he had visualized. For the next hour, he hit different clubs to different targets. Charlie didn't say a word before Jack swung, but asked him to grade his routine after every shot and give feedback on the execution. Occasionally, Charlie offered observations. Sometimes Jack forgot to do his pre-shot waggle; other times, he set his feet before his club and aligned poorly. Charlie also noticed that some swings got a little quick from the top. Almost every time Jack made a poor shot or one that wasn't perfect, he refocused on the routine or a specific part of it and hit a great shot on the next try.

Jack used the feedback from each shot to make adjustments on the next one. Most importantly, Jack didn't hit any disastrous shots. After an hour, Charlie challenged Jack to hit five shots in a row where his only goal was to execute his routine as well as possible.

"We're going to hit five shots to five different targets with five different clubs. If you can grade your routine as an A on three out of the five shots, we'll take this to the golf course."

Jack couldn't wait to test himself where it counted, so he narrowed his focus. Charlie encouraged him to talk his way through each routine and give feedback after each shot.

The first shot was a pitching wedge. Jack described every step clearly, lined up well, swung with great tempo, and hit it straight at the flag.

"That might be the best routine and execution of the day—that's an A!"

The second shot was a 7-iron. Jack talked his way through the routine again, but the shot was a big push.

"I'm going to be honest. My routine was good, but over the ball, I lost focus. I thought that I only needed two more really good routines, and we'd go to the course."

"Great awareness, Jack. Use that as a reminder on the next shot to focus only on the shot at hand."

The next shot was a 5-iron. It started a little lower than Jack had imagined, but it was struck solidly and ended up about twenty feet from the target.

"The routine was good. It was a little low, but I know how much harder it is to hit a 5-iron, so I'm pleased—that's an A."

The next shot was a hybrid. It was quick and ended up being a low pull.

"I didn't really feel the tempo in my practice swing, and I felt out of sync at impact. I'm going to really feel it on this last shot."

"It all comes down to this, Jack. Lots of pressure on this shot with your driver. It's the toughest club in the bag to hit. Don't choke, or you'll have to start again," Charlie said, to try to get in Jack's head. "If you commit to achieving the best routine of the five shots, fully connect to the target, and swing with great tempo without steering it, I'm 100% confident you'll hit an amazing shot."

Jack felt the tension in his body and mind, but took a deep breath and refocused. He made his mind go to the shot at hand, talked his way through his routine, aligned perfectly, stared at his target, and let the moment of calm wash over him. It was as if the swing just happened. Jack's rhythm and balance were perfect. The ball shot off the clubface, started left of the target, and fell gently to the right, landing on the far green he was aiming at, about 270 yards away.

Jack admired the shot and broke into a massive smile. "That felt effortless, so free over the ball. I didn't think about needing to hit a good one. Every thought and action was productive, and it was like I knew I was going to hit a great shot before I ever started the swing. That was so easy, and I'm really proud of how I handled the pressure."

"That was great, Jack. You proved something to yourself, didn't you? You proved that if you do everything, that's in your control, it's much easier to perform under stress. When you fully commit to your routine and process, it blocks out a lot of bad thoughts and memories of poor shots. But when you don't, those thoughts affect your actions and performance. That proves how powerful the routine is. Now you've got to commit to using this approach on the course, on every shot, chip, and putt. It's going to be difficult to achieve that over four or five hours, but the more you practice it, the easier it'll become. You'll hit more good shots, and more importantly, you'll hit fewer bad ones, especially under pressure."

"This is going to be a work in progress. If you put your energy into this during practice for the next two weeks before the State Junior, you'll give yourself the best chance to perform well against a really strong field."

"I know that field is always full of future college players, and college coaches always show up to watch potential recruits. When we get to the course, we'll focus heavily on the routine. But just as important, we'll learn how to give ourselves the best chance by paying attention to what we do, how we think, and how we react between shots. If we practice awareness and learn tools to refocus, you'll be amazed at how transformative it'll be to your game, especially in tournaments." Charlie clapped Jack on the back.

Jack cast his mentor an appreciative smile and nodded.

Strengthen Your Game

1. Why does a productive routine put you more in control and help you stay in the present?

2. Why is it important to ask yourself objective questions after each shot?

3. How do realistic expectations contribute to a balanced mindset during a round?

CHAPTER 9

Taking It to the Course

The sun was lowering in the sky, casting long shadows across the range. Jack wiped the sweat from his brow as he continued to listen to the lessons Charlie was sharing with him.

"We've been out here for a while. Let's finish by playing the first few holes and put that routine into play. We're going to pay a lot of attention to how you react and how you talk to yourself between shots so that you are in the best frame of mind to win the next shot. The important thing for these holes isn't really your score, but the process of how you go about each shot. Let's try to learn the most successful habits you can to help you put them into practice when it counts—when you are on your own in a tournament. Practice these habits just like you have to practice your routine and your swing. The more you practice awareness of what you do in between shots, the quicker it will become a habit. We are going to work on techniques to help overcome unproductive thoughts and actions on the course so you will be as prepared as possible for the next shot, not still thinking about the previous shot."

Jack nodded. "I know I have some bad habits in between shots, but I feel so much better about my routine and the focus it gives me, especially in those moments immediately before I swing. I'm really looking forward to learning more to put me in the most successful mindset before the routine ever starts."

"Great attitude, Jack. So, what do you face here on the first hole?" Charlie gestured toward the hole.

"It's a pretty short par four, so I feel confident I can be successful here. It's 260 yards to the bunker down the right. If I hit my 3-wood, it's right in the landing area, so I'm going to hit my hybrid short of it, which will still leave me about 130 yards. That'll take any stress out of play off the tee, especially bearing in mind it's the first shot of the day, and I might be a bit tight with a 3-wood or the driver."

"I really like that plan, Jack." Charlie gave him a thumbs-up.

Jack went through his routine, connected to his target, and swung with confidence. The ball whistled off the club and faded down the right-center about twenty-five yards short of the bunker.

"How was that routine, Jack?" Charlie asked.

"That was an A. I did everything really well. It was easy to commit to the choice because I knew I couldn't reach the bunker, and my swing felt really free."

"Do me a favor and give yourself an imaginary pat on the back. I want positive reinforcement when you do something really well, so you want to do it again and make it a habit."

Jack nodded and allowed himself a little smile.

"What are you thinking now?" Charlie asked as they walked off the tee.

"I'm going to have a wedge in from there, so I should have a good look at birdie."

"Let's not get too ahead of ourselves and let our minds wander to outcomes. Let's enjoy the walk and widen our focus from golf to something else to relax our mind. What do you want to talk about?"

"Should I not be thinking about that next shot as I'm walking?" Jack's brow scrunched up.

"Whether you're in a good position or a bad position, you'll have plenty of time when you get closer to the ball to figure out your next shot. Right now, let's distract ourselves for a bit. How's school?"

They chatted as they walked down the fairway, and Charlie pointed out a hawk circling over them. "Maybe that's a good sign for a birdie," he joked. As they got within thirty yards of the ball, Charlie said, "Now, let's begin focusing on your next shot. Do you feel nice and relaxed and ready?"

"I really do. Taking my mind off this shot worked. Usually, I think about the last shot, the next one, and what's happening in the round all the way from the tee shot or the iron shot to the next shot."

"I bet doing that on all of those shots in a round makes you feel exhausted by the end of the day, especially if you've hit a bunch of poor shots with all of that thinking and worrying in between." Charlie chuckled softly.

"Some days I just need to lie down when I get home to rest because I'm so tired and emotionally exhausted." Jack joined the easy laughter.

"When you spend so much mental energy thinking about golf all the time in the course of a four-hour round, you wear yourself out. Let's work on finding some other distractions you can try on the golf course after this shot."

"Sounds good to me." Jack grinned.

Jack was 130 yards from the flag, which was on the left side of the green. "Okay. I'm between a wedge and a 9-iron."

Charlie nodded. "Alright, listen, I'm not going to say anything. I'm just here to observe."

Right away, things looked a little different. Jack didn't look committed. His practice swing was quick. Jack set up and hit. It wasn't the nice controlled, balanced swing that he'd grooved over the last couple of hours. The ball started left and nosedived into the greenside bunker.

"This is going to be a really useful learning moment here, Jack. Tell me what happened."

"That was frustrating. I got ahead of myself and started thinking about making a birdie. I went with the hard pitching wedge because it wasn't quite enough club to get all the way to the flag, and now I'm short-sided on an easy par four."

"Remember what I said earlier about not needing to hit every shot pin-high to be able to score?" Jack nodded.

"Well, that flag is in the middle of the green. A normal pitching wedge is going to leave you about fifteen to twenty feet up the hill. That putt is very makeable and would also be a statistically very good shot at the highest levels, let alone in junior golf."

"But I felt like I should try to knock it close. I see what happens when I try to hit a shot that's different from the others I've been practicing. Now I've gone from an easy birdie hole to probably making a bogey. I'm so frustrated with myself; that kind of stuff is what I do in tournaments all the time. I go from being in a good position, then make a poor choice, hit a bad shot, and make a bogey or worse." Jack sighed heavily, staring out at the horizon, not wanting to meet Charlie's gaze.

Charlie placed a steadying hand on Jack's shoulder. "Look, Jack, the thing is, now you know better. If you stay alert and take this lesson to heart, it'll be the best thing that ever happened to you on your learning journey. Go through your thoughts and actions, see what you could have done differently, make a mental note, and move on. Accept the situation. It happens to the best of us. Now, your biggest challenge is to be 100% ready and prepared to hit the best shot that you know you can hit on the next shot. So, let's move on. What other things can you do to distract yourself and relax while you walk to the green?"

Jack grinned slightly. "Well, I like talking about sports. It's cool to look at some of those nice houses on so many courses. I could only dream of living in one of those. I do like wildlife and birds. Every now and again, I'll see a deer in the woods."

"Great. Keep thinking about things just like that. On the next hole, we will talk about some other techniques. Have you gotten over that last shot yet?"

"I have. I'm looking forward to hitting a good bunker shot and trying to give myself a chance to make a miracle par."

"That's the attitude!"

The ball was lying in the flat part of the bunker, four feet below the level of the green. The flag was about fifteen feet from the edge of the green, short-sided, with everything sloping away from Jack. It was a really tough shot.

"How is your bunker play, Jack?"

"I practice all the time, but it's a bit hit and miss."

"So, what are you going to do here?"

"To get it close, I've got to get a load of spin, which means I need speed."

"That's a risky shot, right? If you take that on and hit it a little heavy, it stays in the bunker, and if you hit it a little thin, it goes over the green into the bunker on the other side. I think if you hit it perfectly, you can get it inside ten feet, but there's a lot of risk, isn't there? With risk comes tension and fear, which makes it even more difficult. What would you normally do in a tournament in this situation?" Charlie gave the young golfer an encouraging look.

Jack nodded and cupped his hand to his chin. "Well, if the truth be told, I guess I'd take it on because you have to get it up and down, right? Now I'm not so sure that it's the right shot because I don't feel very confident that I can hit that shot, especially under pressure. I'd be thinking of what could go wrong and make a not very committed swing, which could lead to some terrible results."

"How about if we take the stress out of it and hit it twenty feet past the flag with a normal bunker shot, accept it was a really difficult spot, and know that bogey is a good score, but remove all chances of making a double bogey or worse?" Charlie suggested lightly.

Jack nodded. "I could do that."

"Great. The worst thing you can do is follow up a poor shot with a dumb shot, trying to make up for the previous one. That's where those big numbers come from. I want you to be fully committed to this shot, Jack. Don't just splash it out without focus. Go through your routine, pick a spot you want to land it on, and then hit it. We never want to hit a shot without being fully focused just because it feels like the safe, conservative choice. We're making sure we continue to be fully focused on EVERY shot."

Jack got into the bunker, dug his feet in, looked at where he wanted to land it, and swung. The ball came out beautifully, the sand wedge made that lovely thumping noise, and the ball settled just over twenty feet from the flag.

"Was that where you were trying to hit it?"

"Yes, I did a good job of accepting the situation, and I hit the shot I imagined and committed to."

"Great job! Now this putt is the most important shot. Read it just like you would for a birdie putt and give yourself the best chance for the best result. Think of it as just a twenty-footer; it's no more or less important whether it's a birdie putt or a bogey putt. Let's make the best possible plan we can to give you the very best chance of making the best putt possible. What are your thoughts?"

"I know it's not a putt that I should make, but it's close enough. With a good plan, I could still make it. If not, I'll knock it close enough to two-putt." Jack adjusted his glove.

"Good observation. Tell me your plan."

"It's going to move right to left. It's a little downhill, so it's a little faster than it looks. I can see it starting fairly straight; then it breaks left about ten feet from the hole. I'm going to take a couple of practice swings to feel what I need to do, aim, and stroke it on the line I picked."

"Fantastic plan. Now put it into practice."

Jack went through his routine and rolled it nicely down to the hole. He under-read it just a little, but the pace was perfect, and it ended up a foot away. He tapped it in.

"Great putt, Jack! You did what you needed to do after the poor second shot. You put yourself in a spot where bogey was a good score. Because you stayed focused and shifted your attention to the next shot instead of dwelling on the previous one, you avoided compounding one error with another and avoided the double-bogey. That was a good lesson you learned. Did your reaction feel different from that last tournament?"

"Getting refocused on the routine for the next shot helped me move on and not dwell on that poor second shot. My mind felt clearer, my decision-making was more committed, and my expectations were more realistic. If I'm being honest, I might have tried to make that twenty-footer for a miracle par and risked three-putting." Jack beamed.

Charlie's smile mirrored Jack's. "Good observation. Let's move to the next hole."

Strengthen Your Game

1. How frustrating are those sloppy bogeys from good positions?

2. How could a consistent routine help you reset and avoid compounding mistakes after a bad shot?

3. Based on what you've learned, what strategies can help you stay focused on playing one shot at a time?

CHAPTER 10

Relax Your Body, Free Your Mind

Jack and Charlie walked to the second tee. On the way, Charlie asked Jack another question.

"We've talked about awareness a few times today. Let's talk about awareness of your body and how it feels. Tension is a huge factor that affects performance, especially during competition. If you pay attention to your body right now, are you aware of any tension?"

"I don't really know how to do that," Jack admitted with a shrug.

"When we get to the tee, let's take a minute and open your awareness. Players tend to hold tension in their shoulders in particular—jaws tighten, hands grip the club tighter. When you're tense, you lose a bit of freedom in the swing, and it's difficult to release the club like you do when you're relaxed. That's why you hit a lot of pulls and blocks when you're under pressure and get tight."

They arrived at the tee. The gentle breeze tussled Jack's hair as he closed his eyes and took a moment to try to tap into how his body felt. "My neck and shoulders feel a little tense. One thing I do sense in tournaments is that my chest feels a bit tight. It's an odd feeling, but it's something that feels different from normal."

"That's really typical," Charlie replied. "The tight chest is a symptom of anxiety in competition. You breathe much shallower than normal, and because you don't take in as much oxygen, you take a lot more breaths to get the oxygen your body needs. This sets off alarm bells in your brain that things aren't right. Your brain doesn't work as efficiently, so it's difficult to think and act clearly and decisively. Those moments on the tee when you're waiting or when you're walking to the next shot are really good times to check those tense points in your body. Let's talk about what you can do about that after you hit this next shot."

"Sounds good. Wow, I never realized how connected the mental and physical parts of the game are." Jack gave Charlie a sidelong glance and shook his head slowly.

Charlie couldn't help but chuckle. "No kidding, Jack. No kidding."

The second hole was a challenging par three of over 200 yards. The flag was in a good spot for Jack on the right half of the green.

"Let's check your thought process here," Charlie suggested.

"I know it's a really difficult hole, so a par is a great score. It's 210 yards to the hole, which is in the middle of the green. My 4-iron goes about 200 yards, so if I hit it solid, I'd get on the front third of the green. If I don't quite get all of it, short of the green is fine and is a fairly simple up-and-down. I'm going to aim at the center of the green, start it at the left part of the green, and hit my normal shot."

"I think you're getting the hang of this, Jack. That is really clear thinking, realistic expectations, and exactly what is going to give you the best chance of success."

"I'm not trying to get this all the way to the hole, and I've got to remind myself that a successful shot would be twenty feet short of the flag. I feel good about this one."

Jack went through his routine. Charlie nodded as he locked in with purpose on every step. The rhythm of the routine flowed. It wasn't rushed. One last long look, and Jack let it go. The ball climbed into the sky at the left edge of the green. It was a solid strike, and the ball fell right at the last moment to settle just over the front edge, about forty feet short of the flag.

"That was a really good shot, Charlie. Last week, I would have played that shot differently. I would have swung out of my shoes to force the 4-iron to go another ten yards, and I know I would have pulled it, mishit it, or got out in front of it and missed it way right. Now I understand, based on the yardage and being in between clubs, what a great result that is. I'm really excited to lag it up there and make a great par on a very difficult hole."

"We're making real progress, Jack! Acceptance of situations and their challenges is crucial. That was a perfect example of you doing everything right. Now let's get back to tension and how we deal with it. Once you're aware of tension in a part of your body, an easy fix is to tense that part as tight as you can. Hold that tension for about twenty seconds—you could grip that 4-iron you're holding as tight as you can; feel that tension all the way through your hands, up your arms, and into your shoulders and back. Clench your jaw while you're doing it. Keep squeezing for another fifteen seconds, then release it. You should feel a lot of that tension disappear."

Charlie continued, "I used to do it all the time walking down the fairway or standing on the side of the green waiting to putt. In fact, I won a big tournament by holing an eight-footer after doing that. I knew it was the only way I was going to be free and relaxed enough to make a good stroke under the highest pressure. The more you're aware of the tension, the quicker you can deal with it, so it doesn't become as much of a problem. If you don't have a club, clench your fists and make that extreme tension spread by clenching every muscle, then release them. Does that feel any different now that you've released that stranglehold on the 4-iron?"

"It really does," Jack replied. "I didn't realize how tight I was until you had me practice awareness. Now I feel a little looser and know what to look for, and that has to make my swing freer. How about the tight chest and the breathing?"

"That's something you can practice at home—how to breathe deeper from lower down by your stomach. You'll take in more oxygen, but it takes practice. Then you can start doing it on the course when you're walking, but especially just before you hit a shot or putt. It'll help relax you and help you think much more clearly. One way to help make it a habit is to count your breaths as you walk down the fairway. It helps keep you in the present and focused on a very useful tool. The deeper you breathe, the better prepared you'll be for the next shot."

Jack nodded, taking in every word.

"I'd also count my steps; again, it kept me in the present and helped me move on from the previous shot, so my mind was ready for the next one. Counting breaths and steps is a really good way of achieving that. You'll lose count a lot, but the more you do it, the longer you'll be relaxed, reducing distractions, and put yourself in a great frame of mind to hit the next shot. I'll stop talking—now see if you can count ten deep breaths, and after that, count your steps all the way to the green," Charlie said with a grin.

Jack laughed, then walked to the green, practicing that focus. With a nervous chuckle, he admitted, "I think I lost count a couple of times because I started thinking about the next shot. When I realized that, I started counting again."

"See how those distractions are always trying to get into your head? Counting steps is a really good way to focus intently on something else, which gets you back into the present."

Jack reached the green and looked at his putt. "I feel like I'm really focused as I start my routine. My mind is a lot clearer, which has to be a big advantage over this long putt."

Jack went through his process of reading the putt, judging the slope and break. He pointed out a pitch mark to Charlie and told him the ball needed to just miss it on the left, then pointed out an old hole that he said the ball needed to be really slowing down as it rolled over it to lag it up close.

"Take a really nice, long, slow breath in and release it as you walk into the ball. Now take another one as you look at the target and let it out really slowly as you start the putter back. That's going to calm you down nicely in the stroke."

Jack did exactly what Charlie said. The tempo of the stroke was perfect, and the ball started breaking toward the hole, rolled slowly over the old hole like he imagined, and nestled about two feet from the cup.

"Amazing putt, Jack. How did that feel?"

"So good! That long out-breath as I started the stroke felt like it smoothed out my backswing and led to a great transition and pure roll. I really felt different there—it was like I was on autopilot and everything flowed. The tension was gone."

"That's because you imagined the putt vividly. You were focused and relaxed, and you just reacted to the target. See if you can bottle that feeling!"

"Sounds great! Hey, can I sell it if I manage to bottle it?"

"If you figure out how, then sure. We'll both be millionaires." Charlie chuckled.

They played a few more holes. Jack practiced and focused on his routine, his awareness of his body and mind, and tried to stay as relaxed and tension-free as possible. It was a very different way of playing, with the goal being to pay attention to the things that he could control over everything else.

As they sat down in the grill afterward with a big glass of soda each, Charlie said, "So, give me your feedback about what we did today."

"Charlie, it felt like a game changer. I now realize that I had gotten into the habit of accepting that tournaments are completely different, but that was because I had no control over how I went about things. Now I know that if I can commit to focusing on all the things I can control—from physical routines, to commitment, focus, self-talk, breathing, how I react to situations and bad shots, and how I reduce my tension—it will improve my chances of success in tournaments. I know with the pressure of wanting to do well, the challenges are much greater, but these tools and a new, different direction of where I put my focus will give me the best chance for success. I have two weeks until the biggest tournament of the year. I promise that in those two weeks, my attention will be on what I learned today. I knew I needed to do something—anything—different. My frustration was not knowing what that different direction was. I do now!" He took a long sip of soda, the bubbles tingling in his throat.

"I'm so proud of you, Jack. You opened your mind to a fresh approach, asked the right questions, and quickly took on board what I was saying. You still hit some poor shots, but did you notice that you never hit two poor ones in a row, whether it was on the range or on the course? That will give you the best chance to avoid too many costly bogeys, give you more birdie opportunities, and keep you in contention in every tournament. Spend these next two weeks wisely, and let's catch up the day before the tournament to solidify a few things and help you be as prepared as possible. I think you're going to enjoy competitive golf way more. When you're happier and more in control of yourself, you'll play and score better. Congratulate yourself and use that positive reinforcement to know you're now on the right path."

They clinked glasses to celebrate a great day.

"We're already there, Jack. Just one more topic."

"Oh, what's that?" Jack asked, trying to think of what they hadn't covered.

"How to avoid negative self-talk, especially when things are going well."

Jack couldn't help but laugh. "Oh, good luck with that one, Charlie. I'm the king of negative self-talk, especially when things aren't going well."

Strengthen Your Game

1. Where do you feel tension in your body when you're anxious?

2. How does physical tension influence your swing and mental clarity during a round?

3. If you implement the lessons learned so far, how much more in control will you be when it counts?

CHAPTER 11

The Power of Positive Self-Talk

"One last thing Jack, let's talk about that voice in your head when you're out on the course," Charlie began. "A lot of golfers don't realize how powerful it is. Every thought either builds you up or breaks you down. You've got to train your self-talk to be your biggest ally, not your worst enemy."

Jack nodded, recalling all the times those negative thoughts had messed with his head in big moments. "I get it. I'd be in a tournament, and suddenly, I'd hear stuff like, 'Don't blow it,' or 'What if I miss?' Next thing I knew, I was spiraling."

"Exactly," Charlie agreed. "Remember what we talked about in the clubhouse? Negative self-talk tightens you up, and that tension wrecks your swing and messes with your decision-making. But here's the good news: You're in control of what that voice says. You can flip those negative thoughts into something that actually helps."

"But how do I catch it in the middle of a round?" Jack asked. "When the pressure's on, it's tough to stop those thoughts from taking over."

"It's just like anything else—it takes practice," Charlie said. "Start by paying attention to what you're telling yourself. When those negative thoughts creep in, don't fight them—just catch them, then shift to something positive."

Jack leaned in, ready to dive deeper. "So, what do I say instead?"

"Sure," Charlie said. "Say you're lining up a crucial putt and think, 'What if I miss?' Instead of letting that freak you out, you can tell yourself, 'I've nailed this putt in practice a hundred times—I've got this.' Or, if you're stressing on a drive, ditch the thought 'Don't hit it out of bounds' for 'Pick a clear target and swing with freedom.'"

Jack imagined how much better his game would feel if he could flip the mental switch like that every time. "I see how that changes everything. It's like going from doubt to belief in an instant."

"You got it," Charlie said, smiling. "It's all about owning the story in your head. When you mix positive self-talk with the routines we've drilled, your confidence will start building on its own. You'll step up to each shot knowing you've already set the stage for success. Let's spend a few more minutes together and work on that voice in your head."

They left the clubhouse and strolled over to the practice green, where Charlie lined up some tricky putts for Jack. As Jack took his stance, Charlie stood nearby, ready to coach his mindset.

"Okay, Jack," Charlie said, "tune in to what's running through your head as you line this up. If anything, negative sneaks in, catch it and flip it to something positive. Let's start with this twenty-footer. What's the first thought you're having?"

Jack zeroed in on the putt and immediately caught himself thinking, *This is a tough one—what if I leave it short?* He quickly switched his self-talk. *I've drained putts like this before. Just lock in on the line and the speed.*

Jack locked into his routine, staying dialed in on confidence and execution. He stroked the putt with a smooth, steady rhythm, watching as the ball tracked straight toward the hole and dropped in at the last second.

"Great job!" Charlie said, nodding in approval. "Feels different when your mind's on your side, doesn't it?"

Jack grinned, confidence surging through him. "Yeah, it's like I'm done fighting against myself. Now, I'm just locked in on making it happen."

They spent the next thirty minutes working on putts and chip shots, with Jack zeroing in on catching and flipping any negative self-talk. Each time he nailed it, his confidence grew, knowing he was mastering one of the toughest parts of the mental game.

By the end of the session, Jack was holing more putts and feeling mentally tougher. He knew that with enough practice, this skill would become automatic—his go-to weapon in the clutch.

Charlie carefully pulled out a wrinkled folder, its edges soft from years of use. He flipped it open and handed a printed sheet of paper to Jack. "This has been my go-to for a long time," he said, his voice serious. "A friend from the tour gave me this when we both started giving lessons."

Jack looked at the sheet and quietly read through the list.

When Jack finished, Charlie leaned closer, tapping the paper with his finger. "If you stick to these," he said, "it'll change how you talk to yourself—and that changes how you handle pressure."

Keys to Effective Self-Talk

Self-Talk is a choice: What you say to yourself is under your control. Automatic negative thoughts will come into your mind, but you choose whether to listen to them or replace them. *Don't believe everything you think!*

Awareness is crucial: After a bad shot, it's natural to have negative self-talk. Catch it early and flip it around. Change negative statements like "I can't do anything right today" to positive ones like "I've done it before; I can do it right now."

Focus on what you want to see happen instead of what you are afraid of: Instead of saying, "Don't hit it in the water," say, "Hit your spot on the fairway." Instead of saying, "Don't leave this putt short," say, "Roll it into the back of the cup!" Immediately visualize doing exactly what you want to have happen.

Avoid toxic phrases: Phrases like "I can't" or "I won't" are instant confidence killers. Elite athletes have learned to eliminate these phrases. You can too.

Use silent bragging: Pump yourself up by telling yourself how good you are. Reflect on your successful moments and remind yourself that you can perform well.

Treat yourself like your best friend: After a mistake, talk to yourself the same way you would talk to your best friend. Avoid beating yourself up.

> **If you've done it before, you can do it again:** Remind yourself that any behavior you've done can be repeated. If you've performed well before, you can do it again. Expect to play well!

"Don't forget, Jack," Charlie said, "your mind's either your best ally or your worst enemy—it's all up to you. Keep drilling that positive self-talk until it's a habit, and you'll watch your confidence grow every time you hit the course. The amazing thing is positive self-talk will help you in all parts of your life."

"Thanks, Charlie! These are great!" Jack said, his eyes fixed on the sheet.

He knew the mental edge he was building would give him a real shot at outplaying the competition. With every practice, he wasn't just getting better at the physical game of golf but the mental game, too. He was determined to let his inner voice be all about belief, confidence, and strength. The thing that stood out most to Jack was that everything they worked on today was putting him more in control of his thoughts and actions.

Strengthen Your Game

1. Reflecting on your last tough round, how would you describe your self-talk?

2. List examples of negative self-talk and practice, reframing each one into something positive.

3. Can you commit to staying mindful of your self-talk through every challenge on the course?

Timeline of a Strategic Routine

Pre-shot
  -Commit fully
  -Visualize vividly
  -Feel intentionally

Shot
  -Set up consistently
  -Connect to the target
  -React to the target
  -Swing athletically and intuitively

Post-shot
  -Objective reaction
  -Did I do everything in my control?
  -What could I have done better?
  -Learn and move on

Walk
  -Distract from overthinking/ overanalyzing
  -Breathing to calm the mind
  -Reduce tension in the body
  -Positive self-talk

CHAPTER 12

Confidence Is Built on Preparation

It had been two weeks since Jack saw Charlie. But today was the day before the State Junior, and Jack wanted to talk with Charlie about his golf game. As the sun peeked through the window, they sipped on their drinks.

"So, how have the last couple of weeks been?" Charlie asked. "Have you noticed a difference?"

Jack's eyes lit up. "Charlie, it's been a really cool experience preparing completely differently from what I'd usually do. I used to just hit a bunch of balls every day, chip and putt for hours at a time, then hope it would build confidence. It was a bit of a pattern. A day or two before most tournaments, I'd struggle with my swing and try to hit more balls to practice my way out of it. But I'd just make things worse, get frustrated, and lose confidence. This past week has felt very different. I still practiced, but hit fewer balls with more focus, so I gained confidence in my swing without wearing myself out. I still hit some poor ones, but it didn't bother me as much and helped me refocus better on the next shot. When I went on the course, I was less focused on my score and concentrated fully on the process we worked on."

Jack raised his eyebrows. "By the way, my scores got better, and I made fewer bogeys each round. I really believe in what we've begun, but I know I have to keep working on it to make it even better in the long run."

"Fantastic! You're a far different player than you were when we first met," Charlie said, a glint in his eye.

"The main thing I feel right now is that I can't wait to put this into practice tomorrow—stay committed even when things go wrong—and learn from the experience so I can do better next time. I'm paying attention to my self-talk, being more aware of tension, focusing on what to do during the walk between shots, and committing fully to my pre-shot routine. I've never felt like this the day before a tournament. It feels like I have an ace up my sleeve compared to everyone else." Jack's self-confidence was high as he faced what was ahead.

Charlie pointed at Jack and smiled. "There's not much else I can say to add to that. You'll notice the bad habits in others, the things you used to do in tournaments. Use those things as a reminder to give yourself a pat on the back for the work you've put in. You're a different golfer, a golfer who now has a great routine and mindset and knows how to use them."

Jack nodded, a broad smile breaking across his face.

"One last thing, Jack. Tournament golf is all about handling the tough times and adversity that will happen during the round. If you can use what we've learned and save shots during those challenging times, you can transform your round with one forty-five-minute stretch of great play. When you trust and believe in yourself and your preparation, a round can completely flip within two or three holes. Hang in there, believe in yourself, and trust in your process—you now have the tools to fulfill your potential in tournament play.

"Tomorrow is still going to feel uncomfortable; embrace that feeling of nerves, anxiety, and excitement. Things will go wrong in the round—people will try to get in your head, you'll get bad breaks and bounces, and you'll make the odd poor decision or get distracted by the score or a poor shot. In every one of those situations, use it as a cue to get straight back to your process: your routine, your breathing, staying in the present, and releasing tension. Don't let your mind wonder about the 'what-ifs,' play the course, not the competition. If you can do a good job of that, you'll do great. Here's a reminder of your goals that will give you the best chance of success tomorrow," Charlie said as he handed Jack a scribbled a note on the back of a scorecard.

Jamesville Municipal
Est. 1952

C–A–L–M

<u>C</u>ommit to your process

<u>A</u>wareness of your thoughts and body

<u>L</u>et go of what already happened

<u>M</u>ake the next shot the most important one

10284 Lattasburg Rd.
Jamesville, SC 29020
(803) 612-2726

"I wish you the best of luck; you've done all the hard work. Now go and enjoy the tournament. Have a good dinner, get a good night's sleep, and get ready for an amazing day tomorrow."

Jack finished his drink and shook Charlie's hand. "Thank you so much, Charlie. I can't thank you enough—I'm really looking forward to the challenge. I'm more ready than I've ever been."

Strengthen Your Game

1. Why is it essential to focus only on what you can control before a critical round?

2. Make a list of things you can control versus those you can't during a round.

3. Why do you think mental preparation is as important as physical training before a big round?

CHAPTER 13

Showtime: Perform When It Matters

Morning sunlight sparkled on the dew-covered grass as Jack approached the clubhouse, his heart pounding with each step. This was the big one, the South Carolina State Junior, the tournament that could change everything. Tension buzzed in the air. This wasn't just a tournament; it was Jack's chance to prove he could hang with the best in the state, with college scouts and coaches tracking every swing. The pressure was real, but Jack told himself he was ready.

Jack pushed open the clubhouse door and stepped into a whirlwind of chatter. His gaze zeroed in on his rival, Nick, lounging in a chair, with a group of players. Nick oozed confidence, as if he'd already won. With perfectly styled hair, a crisp polo, and that unmistakable future pro swagger, Nick was the golden boy of junior golf.

Nick's eyes met Jack's, a sly grin creeping across his face. "Ready for another lesson, Sullivan?" His words dripped with sarcasm. "Check the board. It's you and me again. We're out first, so you might want to get ready."

Jack's heart raced, but he wasn't letting Nick slither into his thoughts. He took a deep breath, replaying Charlie's advice: *Play the course, not the competition.* He exhaled slowly, letting the tension drain away.

"I'm looking forward to it," Jack replied.

Jack's warm-up on the range built on the confidence from the past two weeks. He committed to his routine before each swing. Not only did this lead to swings that were in control, but, perhaps more importantly, it engaged his mind fully on what was to come on the course. It was a completely different feeling than previous tournaments. Jack was ready!

As Jack headed to the putting green, confidence surged through him. Charlie's mental game lessons anchored him, steadying his nerves. Each short putt clicked into the cup. The pace on his longer putts was beautiful. The clubhouse noise faded; it was just him and the green. There was an inner calm, a sense of control, and deeper trust in his game.

The crowd around the first tee was bigger than usual, with parents, coaches, and curious onlookers eager to see how the state's top golfers would perform. The announcer's voice boomed over the loudspeaker: "Next on the tee, from Westview High School—Jack Sullivan."

Jack stepped up to the tee box, wiping his sweaty palms on his pants before locking in on his routine - *Commit, visualize, feel, and target.* The fairway stretched out, tree-lined and dotted with bunkers, waiting for a misstep. He took one last deep breath, let it out, and swung.

The driver cracked against the ball, launching it straight down the fairway. Relief washed over him as the ball settled perfectly where he wanted it. A grin tugged at his lips—he was off to a strong start.

"Nice shot," Nick said, his voice heavy with mock sincerity.

Jack stayed silent, determined to keep his focus locked on his own game. Nick was a pro at mind games, but Jack wasn't biting today. It was just him and the course—nothing else mattered.

Nick unleashed a powerful drive, sending the ball just past Jack's, but it veered slightly into the rough. As they walked the fairway, Charlie's advice echoed in Jack's mind: *Stay in the moment. Win this shot.*

Jack's approach shot was clean, the ball floating softly onto the green, settling eight feet from the pin. Nick hit a fantastic second shot out of the rough. His ball rolled to within six feet of the hole. Tension hung in the air. Moments like this had rattled Jack before, but not today. He was determined to stick to his game plan.

As he lined up his putt, familiar doubts whispered in his ear: *What if you miss? What if Nick sinks his and grabs the lead?* Jack shook them off and flipped the script. *You've drained putts like this a hundred times in practice. You're rolling it great. Trust your routine.* He took a deep breath, locked onto his line, and sent the ball rolling smoothly toward the hole. It fell dead center.

The small crowd around the green offered polite applause, but inside, Jack gushed with confidence. He was in control, and nothing else mattered. Nick made his putt as well, and they moved to the next hole, both sitting at one under par.

The next few holes went by in a blur of smooth swings and focused putts. Jack felt like he was in the zone—his mind clear, his body relaxed. He wasn't thinking about Nick, the score, or the college scouts watching. He was just playing golf, one shot at a time. By the time they reached the sixth hole, Jack was two under and tied for the lead. Nick trailed at one under, but Jack could sense the frustration simmering beneath the surface. Nick wasn't used to trailing—especially not to Jack.

Jack's tee shot on the seventh hole was his best of the day.

Nick's frustration boiled over. "You're playing out of your mind, Sullivan," he muttered. "But let's see if you hold up when the real pressure kicks in. Remember the last tournament?"

Jack didn't take the bait. He knew exactly what Nick was doing and used Nick's mind games as a reminder to stay locked in on his routine. *Play the course, not Nick.*

Nick's drive was solid, but his second shot missed the green, leaving him with a tricky chip that he chunked.

Jack stayed cool, sticking his approach to six feet and calmly draining the birdie putt. After tapping in for bogey, a frustrated Nick gave Jack a dirty look. For the first time in a long while, Jack felt like he had the upper hand—not just on the scorecard, but in the mental game as well.

By the time they finished the ninth hole, Jack was three under par and tied for fourth in the tournament. As he saw his name near the top, excitement buzzed in Jack's chest. He could hear Charlie's voice prompting him to play one shot at a time. *Plenty of golf left. Just win this next shot.*

The back nine had always been Jack's biggest challenge. In past tournaments, he had started strong, only to crumble under the pressure when things got tight. He could feel the familiar tension creeping in as he walked to the tenth tee.

Nick must've sensed it, too. He leaned in, voice low and taunting, "This is where you always blow it, Sullivan. Let's see if you can keep it together this time."

Jack gritted his teeth and took a slow, steady breath, forcing himself to block out Nick. But as he set up for his drive, doubt crept in. *What if he's right?*

As he hovered over the ball longer than usual, Jack felt Nick's stare. His grip tightened, and his swing was tight and rushed. The result was exactly what he dreaded—a weak slice into the rough. It was the first shot all day he had regretted. Jack had let the distractions affect him.

"I should have backed off that one with all those bad thoughts swirling around my head and started again," Jack muttered.

And just like that, his game started to unravel. Jack's second shot clipped a tree and landed short of the green. His third shot buried itself in a bunker, the pressure piling on with every step. By the time he walked off the green, he'd carded a double bogey, knocking him back to one under. Nick, meanwhile, calmly parred the hole.

Frustration crashed over Jack like a wave. *You blew it again. You're choking—just like Nick said you would.* But then he pulled himself back. Charlie's voice echoed in his head: *One bad hole doesn't define your round. Just win this next shot.*

Jack saw Matt by the green. "That was the old Jack on that last hole. I let the situation and negative thoughts get the better of me and lost my clear thinking. Don't worry, Matt," he said with a wink and a grin, "the new Jack is in charge," as he confidently walked to the next tee.

Jack took a few steady breaths as he slung his bag over his shoulder. He reached into his back pocket and pulled out the scorecard Charlie gave him yesterday. He used it as an immediate reminder of the goals they talked about.

Jack sensed this was the period Charlie had talked about, where he had to hang in there after that gut punch on ten, right the ship, and trust that forty-five minutes of great play would transform his round. He knew that in the past, what happened on ten would have led to that spiral—not today!

Slow it down. Stick to the routine—just like in practice. Trust your swing. One shot at a time. I'll worry about the score when it's all over.

The tee shot wasn't perfect, but still found the short grass. Jack felt more in control, but as was his tendency under stress, he got a bit quick and pulled his approach shot—another bogey. He was now back to even par and knew the round was slipping away. Could he regain that calmness? Could he regain the momentum that saw him shoot three-under on the front nine?

Once again, Jack went to the side of the tee on twelve, closed his eyes, took some deep breaths, tensed his body, and released. He knew that his self-talk had gotten a little off track. Bringing himself back to the present, Jack told himself, "You are playing great. One bad hole or a few shaky swings will not ruin a good day. Back to my routine. Let's finish strong." Jack sensed he was turning the corner.

After a mediocre drive on twelve, Jack had 180 yards to the hole, with a front-left flag—a really tough pin position for him normally, but especially after what had just happened on ten and eleven. Jack had to find a way to hit a solid shot. He tensed his body as tight as he could, held it, and then let it go after thirty seconds. He knew short and right wasn't a bad miss, so he committed to a 6-iron aimed at the center of the green, knowing it wouldn't get to pin high, but if he could hit it decently, it would give him his best chance of making par. Trying to block out everything that happened on ten and eleven, Jack set about seeing and feeling the shot—this was a pivotal moment in his round.

The swing was a little quick; it was a bit of a push, and the ball floated high and a little right, but in a spot where he knew he could get up and down. *That's the best mis-hit ever!* Jack thought. *Now let's get ready to hit the best chip of the day when I get to my ball.* Jack strolled to the green, more relaxed and freer, and looked at the beautiful blue sky, noticing a squirrel running across the fairway into the woods. He felt in control, eager to win the next shot.

Jack stared at his ball. The lie was perfect, and he visualized the shot—a fairly simple chip-and-run with a nine-iron. Jack surveyed the shot, picked his landing spot, which was very close to the edge of a shadow creeping onto the green. The practice swing was rhythmical and felt great. Jack was in control of the situation. *Click*—the ball came off the clubface, landed a few inches from the shadow, and started rolling like a putt right at the hole, pulling up twelve inches short. What a shot! Jack smiled, knowing he was back in control.

Confidence built as he walked to the thirteenth tee, the toughest par-three on the course. It was fairly long at 190 yards, with a small green full of ridges and slopes. After the chip on twelve, Jack sensed he was almost back to where he was on the front nine. Full focus was needed here. With a 5-iron in hand, Jack knew par was a great score and set about figuring out the best plan for the shot. The center of the green was the right choice, giving himself a bit of wiggle room. He saw the soft fade, but this time reminded himself to really let the club set at the top of the backswing. The practice swing felt amazing. He set up, looked at the target, and let it go. The ball soared into the air and landed right in the center of the green. Jack gave a little fist pump to congratulate himself on a great shot and remind himself to stay positive.

It was a very difficult putt, up and over a two-foot-high ridge. Jack read the putt, saw it running up and over the slope, picking the high point. The practice stroke felt good, and he stroked it. The putt looked good, but picked up speed and ran five feet past. Jack could hear Charlie's words from his self-talk list: *I've done this thousands of times before. I'm in control of myself. Let's roll this in the cup.* Jack composed himself, took a couple of deep breaths, and settled in. The putt was dead straight. He felt relaxed. The routine flowed, and he rolled it right into the center.

There was a sense of inevitability about the putt. Jack was back to the relaxed feel of the front nine. He smoked the tee shot on fourteen right down the middle. Jack sensed that this was the start of that forty-five minutes Charlie had talked about.

Jack recalled how Charlie told him to count his steps and his breaths as he walked from one hole to the next. With a steadying breath, Jack briefly closed his eyes and focused, forcing himself to visualize Charlie's kind eyes and hear his encouraging voice. When Jack opened his eyes, he stared straight ahead and counted under his breath, first his steps until he reached ten, then his breaths for ten. He switched back and forth until arriving at the next shot. By the time he reached his destination, thoughts of failure and Nick were far away.

Nick, meanwhile, was unraveling. A missed three-foot putt on hole eleven led to three straight bogeys. Jack watched as Nick slammed his putter into his bag, muttering under his breath, "What's happening? You're falling apart. You're letting this slip away."

Who's blowing it now? Jack thought while fighting to keep a straight face.

By the fifteenth hole, Jack was clearly back to playing his best golf. The crowd, the leaderboard, even Nick, blurred into the background. It was just him, trusting his swing. His drive was pure, splitting the fairway and leaving him with a perfect approach shot. The second shot nestled just a few feet from the hole, setting up a tap-in birdie to get back to under par for the day.

Rattled by Jack's steady play and his struggles, Nick missed his birdie putt and grudgingly settled for par. The gap between their scores grew wider.

On the sixteenth hole, Nick buckled under pressure. His drive splashed into the water, panic flashing across his face. Jack played it smart, sticking to a safe drive and a steady approach that left him with a routine par. Meanwhile, Nick stumbled to a double bogey, sliding even further behind.

Walking to the seventeenth tee, Jack ignored Nick's growing frustration. Nick's confidence had vanished, and his frustration showed on every poor shot. But instead of getting swept up in thoughts of beating Nick, Jack locked onto his routine. *Just win this shot.*

The seventeenth was a long par-three—water left, bunkers fronting the green. The kind of hole that could make or break a round. Jack stood over his tee shot, picturing the ball soaring high and dropping softly onto the green. He released his breath, swung easily, and watched as the ball traced the exact path he'd imagined. Right on target. His heart skipped as the ball landed dead center on the green, rolling closer to the pin.

Could it be a hole-in-one? The thought flashed through his mind. Jack shook his head and grinned as the ball stopped just inches short.

Nick's silence was telling—his brows knitted, jaw clenched. He stomped over to his bag and grabbed a different club; the pressure weighed heavy on his shoulders. A rushed backswing sent his shot straight into the deep left-front bunker. He slammed his club into his bag and hurried off the tee box. Nick would eventually settle for another bogey.

Heading to the eighteenth hole—a long par-five with danger lurking on both sides—Jack reminded himself: *Stick to your routine. Play your game.*

Nick, desperate and spiraling, went for broke, aiming to reach the green in two. But his aggressive play backfired. The second shot caught the wind and drifted into the deep rough, barely staying in bounds. Nick slashed it onto the green. He rolled his first putt well past the hole, and then he three-putted from there for a crushing double bogey. It was clear he had completely given up.

Jack played it smart, laying up with his second shot to leave himself a comfortable wedge in. A smooth swing sent the ball flying straight toward the pin, landing softly fifteen feet short and gently trickling within twelve feet.

The crowd hushed as Jack stepped up to his ball. That old enemy, his nerves, crept in, but he shoved them aside. *This is just like practice. You've got this.*

He took a deep, steady breath, focused on the line, and stroked the putt. It tracked perfectly, catching the right edge and dropping in. The crowd erupted, and Jack finally exhaled in relief.

As they walked off the green, Nick tried to mask his frustration, but the anger in his eyes was unmistakable. "You got lucky today, Sullivan," he muttered as he slung his clubs onto his back.

Jack didn't bite. He knew now that success wasn't about luck. It was about staying mentally sharp, even when everything felt shaky. "It's not luck, Nick," Jack said, his voice calm. "It's about controlling what you can control. Maybe you should try that."

Nick scowled and stormed off, but Jack barely noticed. He was proud—not just of his score, but of how he'd handled the pressure. He stuck to his plan, blocked out the noise, handled adversity, and finished strong.

When the final scores were posted, Jack shot sixty-nine and saw he'd tied for sixth out of 120 players. It was the best finish and the lowest tournament score of his young career. Nick, after his back-nine collapse, wound up in ninety-fifth.

Leaving the course, Jack couldn't stop grinning. He knew there was still a lot of work ahead, but today proved he had what it took to compete with the best. The road was still long, but Jack was up for the challenge. He wasn't just playing golf anymore—he was mastering the mental game, one shot at a time.

Strengthen Your Game

1. From Jack's tournament experiences, what key lessons apply to your own game?

2. What advice would you share with Nick based on your learning and experiences?

3. When you hit a rough patch, what helps you hang in until the momentum shifts?

4. Reflect on your last competitive round. How would you approach things differently now?

CHAPTER 14

This Changes Everything

Jack walked away from the scorer's table after double and triple-checking his scorecard. He still couldn't believe how well he'd done. His parents, Matt, and Charlie were waiting for him to congratulate him on his impressive performance. They had all looked at the scoreboard and saw how many players he had beaten who were already committed to playing Division-1 college golf.

While hugging his parents and giving high-fives to Matt and Charlie, he saw Nick rushing to his shiny new car that he got for his sixteenth birthday last week. He popped the trunk open and chucked his golf bag in, then tossed his shoes in as hard as he could, slamming the trunk shut. The car roared to life, and the tires screeched as he sped away as quickly as he could.

"That's a shame. I hope Nick didn't snap any clubs when he threw them in the trunk," Matt joked.

"It's odd. I actually feel a bit sorry for him, even though he's never been nice to me. I think his confidence is so fragile, and a day like he had today is going to sting for a long time," Jack said.

"Let's not worry too much about him, Jack," Charlie said. "Just focus on you and what you were able to accomplish. You were amazing out there today. You beat a lot of fantastic older players with college careers ahead of them."

A smile stretched across Jack's face.

Charlie put his hand on Jack's shoulder. "You were in control of your game, your emotions, and your preparation for each shot. Even when you had that sticky patch on the back nine, you hung in there, gave yourself a chance to finish strong, and posted that amazing score on a really tough golf course. I could see you refocus, especially after bad shots—you hit really smart shots to minimize the damage and never followed up a poor shot with a dumb one. I kept noticing you working on releasing tension while walking down the fairways. I enjoyed watching you play. What was it like for you?"

"First, I was nervous, but I didn't let it get out of control where I couldn't think or play well. I knew I had a plan and tools to help me under the stress of today. Before, my nerves would've gotten the best of me, and I would've cracked under the pressure. When things went wrong, I consciously went back to my routine and everything we worked on. I got things back on track."

Jack took his cap off and wiped his forehead. "I can't believe how relaxed I was over those last few holes, and making those birdies at the end was a nice bonus. It's the best tournament I've ever played, against the strongest field of older, better players. I now believe I belong with the big boys! You know what? One thing surprised me. I didn't play perfectly, I just played smart and in the moment. Apart from the one double-bogey, I took care of the par fives and saved a lot of shots from tough positions. I've heard it before from the players on TV about not needing to play perfectly to be successful—now I understand what they were talking about."

There was a lot of excited talking and laughing from Jack and his group; it was the happiest and most enthused he'd ever been after a tournament round of golf. He didn't notice another person join the group.

"Hi, Jack. I just wanted to introduce myself and congratulate you on a great day. My name is Coach Clifton from Carolina State. I'm the head golf coach there and wanted to tell you how impressed I was watching you. I saw you doing things that I try to teach my players on the team. The successful ones get it and take it on board, but some never do and end up not playing very much. I saw you working on your deep breathing and releasing tension on twelve tee to reset. You played smart golf — you had a very repeatable and productive routine, and it looked like you were in control of yourself."

Jack smiled. "Thanks!"

The coach continued, "Oh, and another thing that really stood out to me was your body language when things weren't going well. You gave the impression that nothing bothered you. Lots of kids' shoulders slump when things don't go well—they complain, speed up, or really slow down, and things usually spiral from there. I noticed you gave yourself a little fist pump after the tee shot on thirteen—I love positive reinforcement! You made some really mature, smart decisions, which allowed you to stay in the round and keep your score manageable, giving you a chance to post a great number with that really impressive finish."

"Why haven't I had you on my radar yet?" Coach Clifton asked with a chuckle.

Jack shrugged and laughed.

"Well, no matter. I'll be keeping a close eye on you and your results from now on, Jack. You're just the kind of player who could help my team in the future. Keep making progress—you're going to be a junior next year, right?"

"Yes, sir," a dumbstruck Jack replied.

Coach Clifton was a legend in the state, and every local kid wanted to be on his team.

"Keep up the great work, Jack," Coach Clifton shook Jack's hand before the coach walked towards the clubhouse.

"Wow, thank you." Jack was starstruck, watching as the coach grew smaller in the distance.

"Well, that might be the cherry on top of an amazing day." Charlie grinned, holding out his hand to Jack.

Jack shook Charlie's hand. "It might be the best day of my golfing life. It feels like the first day of the next chapter of my sporting life. I have a great plan. I have a great approach that'll separate me from my competition, and I can't wait to see what the future holds. And I have you to thank, Charlie."

"Anytime, Jack, anytime. You proved that when you commit to a process and are in control, you give yourself the best chance of success. Instead of hoping to play well, you now have the tools to play your best in competition."

Jack grinned. "I can't wait for the next tournament. This changes everything."

Strengthen Your Game

1. What qualities do you think college coaches notice most in a player?

2. Could adopting Jack's new approach help you enjoy golf more and feel less pressure?

3. How will you use post-round feedback to prepare better for your next round?

About the Authors

Gary Christian

With over thirty years of experience in the game of golf, Gary Christian has built a career that spans from the competitive fairways to the broadcast booth. He now focuses on helping golfers of all levels master the art of scoring. A standout player during his NCAA Division 1 career at Auburn University, he earned All-SEC honors in 1994. As a professional, Gary went on to secure thirty wins on various mini-tours and two victories on the Korn Ferry Tour.

Gary's journey to the PGA Tour is one of remarkable perseverance. At forty, he became one of the oldest true rookies in modern PGA Tour history. He credits his dedication to both the mental and physical sides of the game as the catalyst to his success as a professional golfer.

For the past decade, Gary has become a trusted voice in the world of golf commentary, covering the top players as an on-course analyst with the Golf Channel, NBC Sports, ESPN, PGA Tour Live, and SKY Sports. As a PGA of America member, Gary also dedicates his time to coaching golfers, where he focuses on the mental aspects of the game. He helps players unlock their full potential through improved focus, emotional control, and smarter course management.

Whether through his insightful commentary or his coaching, Gary Christian brings a wealth of experience and passion to the game, helping golfers at every level improve their performance and enjoy the sport they love.

Dr. Curt Ickes

Dr. Curt Ickes, a bestselling author and emeritus professor at Ashland University, has over thirty-five years of experience in clinical and sport psychology. He specializes in training athletes in "stop-and-go" sports, such as baseball, golf, softball, and track and field events like throwing and jumping. His passion for the mental side of performance has led him to work with athletes of all levels, from youth leagues to the pros, sharpening their mental skills to achieve peak performance.

Dr. Ickes has served as the sport psychologist for individual athletes and teams. He conducts mental game clinics for coaches and players and continues to work with Ashland University's sports teams. Dr. Ickes is known for his engaging storytelling and practical mental game strategies. His books, including *Win the Next Pitch!*, *Pitch by Pitch!*, and *You Got This!*, have sold over 50,000 copies collectively, helping thousands of athletes develop mental toughness and excel both on and off the field.

Dr. Ickes combines his deep understanding of psychology with practical strategies to equip athletes with the tools they need to succeed and face competition with confidence and resilience.

Contact the authors:
Gary Christian – GaryJChristian@gmail.com
Curt Ickes – Curtickes7@gmail.com

Printed in Great Britain
by Amazon